The Christ of the American Road

E. STANLEY JONES

ABINGDON-COKESBURY PRESS

New York • *Nashville*

THE CHRIST OF THE AMERICAN ROAD
COPYRIGHT, MCMXLIV
By WHITMORE & STONE

1944

Wartime Books

Wartime shortage of pulp, manpower, and transportation has produced a severe shortage of paper. In compliance with orders of the War Production Board, wartime books are printed on lighter-weight paper. This reduces thickness and weight. New books have more words to the page and smaller margins. This reduces the number of pages without reducing reading content.

Thinner books save paper, critical copper, and other metals. They help also to avoid wartime increases in book prices. Wartime books appear to be smaller, but their content has not been cut. They are complete. The only change is in appearance.

THE CHRIST OF THE
AMERICAN ROAD

CONTENTS

ACKNOWLEDGMENT is expressed to Harper and Brothers
for quotations from *The Bible: A New Translation* by James
Moffatt; to The Macmillan Company for material from *The
Rise of American Civilization* by Charles A. and Mary R. Beard;
and to Little, Brown and Company and The Atlantic Monthly
Press for material from *The Epic of America* by James Truslow
Adams. These last two books are sources for most of the data and
quotations from American history in the following pages.

INTRODUCTION

AFTER TWENTY YEARS in India I wrote *The Christ of the Indian Road*. I gave the manuscript to the publisher with an apology and went back to India. I expected nothing from it. Its reception was a surprise to me. When I look back to see the reason for that reception, I think perhaps it was this: it was new to a good many people to find that each nation has something distinctive to contribute to the interpretation of the universal Christ. Seeing Christ in the light of one national interpretation—their own—they took it for granted that this was *the* interpretation, the Truth itself. They were surprised to find that other peoples, with a different racial history and culture, might bring out other phases and emphases of the universal Christ which they had missed. But to some of us who have roamed afar it has become a commonplace that it will take the sons of men to interpret the Son of Man.

For none of us has the Truth. The Truth is in Christ—the Truth. What we hold is truths about the Truth. We need, therefore, the other person's truth to add to our truths, so that our pooled truths may more closely approximate him who is *the* Truth. I say "more closely approximate," for even our pooled truths are forever this side of the Truth. We shall eternally grow into deeper and larger comprehension of the Truth, and assimilate it more and more into character and achievement; that will be our happiness and our heaven.

Each individual and each nation has something distinctive to contribute to the fuller interpretation of the Christ. Just as Paul could say "my gospel"—for it was a gospel that had gone through the cultural history and personality of Paul and was colored by that fact—so each nation has a unique past, and therefore a unique personality, and through that unique personality can give a unique interpretation of Christ. While keeping itself open to other interpretations, and thus taking their corrections, nevertheless each nation must dare be itself, must dare believe that it has a call and a commission to offer humbly to the rest its own interpretation of the Universal Fact. Just as each individual must allow the Spirit of God to pull out the stops and play all over the keyboard of his life, so each nation must present itself to God to be played over so that its notes, definite and distinctive, may be a part of the universal harmony.

When God makes the individual, he breaks the pattern. That individual is one with the rest of humanity, and yet he is sole, unique, different. Through that individual God would open a fresh book of revelation. For that individual can give an interpretation of the manifold God which no one else can give. Through the nation, too, God is desiring to open a fresh book of revelation. The nation may not respond, and that book of revelation may be forever closed and sealed, and because of it the human race will be forever the poorer.

The son of the great Emerson said: "My father picked up many things, not necessarily new, but he colored them."

Introduction

We Americans have picked up many things from all the world, but we have colored them; they are now American. A thoughtful Englishman once said, "I trust I am a Christian Englishman, but I know that I am also an English Christian, and my life has been molded partly by the Christian faith and partly by contemporaneous English society." The same with us. We are Americans, and our lives have been molded partly by the New Testament and partly by American history and culture. That history and culture are unique. Through them God intends to offer a unique offering to the world. That should not make us proud. It should humble us to believe that we can be the instruments of a purpose beyond ourselves, and that a divine purpose. We are a people of destiny. But so are all people. We should take what they have to offer, and then humbly present our own offering.

In many parts of our country the English walnut is grafted on the stump of the American black walnut. The black walnut is indigenous, and for this reason has power to resist local disease and climate. So Christianity is grafted on the root of our American culture and history. That makes our contribution unique.

What that particular offering is, which America has to offer, will be the theme of this book.

I may not have grasped that peculiar contribution of America, but at least I have had a unique opportunity for doing so. I have been living away from America for many years. That is an advantage, for after living abroad you see your country in the total setting of the world. "He who knows only one language doesn't know any"; so he who knows only one country doesn't know any. You must see

9

your country, with all its strengths and weaknesses and short-comings, in contrast. No one has ever really seen the Statue of Liberty who hasn't seen it after a long absence from this land. I can understand the soldier who, after a long absence in the South Seas, on returning to America knelt down and kissed the soil of his homeland. Something goes up and down my spine whenever, after a long time abroad, I sail up the Hudson and see the Statue of Liberty. And if a silent tear of gratitude for the meaning of that statue falls down my cheeks, I let it fall—unashamed.

But just to be away and come back is not enough. You must get under the skin of the situation when you do come back. In none of my previous visits had I ever been able to accomplish that. I talked to America from the outside. I preached *at* her, and most of the preaching was critical. America was not what I had hoped to find her, and I told her so, sometimes in stinging phrases. I never *belonged*. I felt I belonged to the East, and was talking to the West. I felt I must plead for my adopted lands against the wrongs the West had imposed on them.

Now I belong to America—not supremely, of course, for that allegiance is subject to a higher allegiance—but I do belong. This book has been written from the inside, and I'll tell you how I got on the inside: God put me there.

The night before I went off to college to study for the ministry the pastor of the little church where I was brought up and converted preached a sermon on the text: "He that goeth forth and weepeth, bearing precious seed, shall doubt-less come again with rejoicing, bringing his sheaves with him." To my surprise and youthful embarrassment the sermon was about my going away. When I came back from college and was about to sail for India, the pastor preached another sermon on the text, "The Lord shall preserve thy going out, and thy coming in, from this time forth, and even for evermore." Of course to me the emphasis was upon "thy going out"—the adventure of leaving my native land to begin a walk with the Christ of the Indian Road. It did not strike me at all that the emphasis would ever shift to the phrase "thy coming in," that I should ever feel the same tingle of adventure in coming back to my native land, not merely to see loved ones and friends, although that was precious, but to discover and to walk with the Christ of the American Road. But that has happened. I had thrilled to my fingertips in discovering and interpreting the Christ of the Indian Road, and in walking with him. But I have thrilled more deeply—perhaps more mature years have made that possible—as I have awakened to the possibility of the meaning of the Christ of the American Road to this and other lands. *I think I see something.*

My eyes began to open in the following incident. Two months before I was to come back to America for the National Christian Mission, when I was at the Sat Tal Ashram in the Himalayas, out of a clear sky the Inner Voice said, "It's all right; I'll get you there safely and on time." That Voice kept repeating those words. I wondered about it, for I saw no reason for such a persistent assurance. I had my reservation on a French plane from Calcutta to Hong Kong, and from there was to take the "President Coolidge" to San Francisco, which would give me ample time to meet my first engagement in the opening of the Ashram at Saugatuck, Michigan. But I soon found there was reason for that assurance. France collapsed and with it the French air line.

Then I obtained a reservation on an Italian boat, but Italy got into the war, and that was out. My last hope was a reservation on a Japanese steamer calling at India, which would get me to Hong Kong in time to get the clipper across the Pacific. But the Mediterranean closed when Italy got into the war, and this steamer could not get through. Everything fell to pieces. Possibilities of going East or West were sealed.

Two days before I sailed I hadn't a possibility, and yet the Voice persisted, "It's all right; I'll get you there safely and on time." So I was inwardly calm and assured, for the Voice had never let me down. Two days before I sailed I was informed that an American steamer was sailing from Bombay via South Africa to New York. I found on arrival at Bombay that the steamer would take forty days for the trip, and forty days would not get me there on time, and the Voice had said, "Safely and *on time*." Still it was the only thing open, and I took it. In South Africa we were held up a further three days, which would make me ten days late. Still I was calm and assured, and was able to give undivided attention to the finishing of the manuscript of *Is the Kingdom of God Realism?*

After sailing from South Africa the captain announced that he would have to stop in Trinidad, West Indies, for oil and water. I found Trinidad was on the line of the clippers to South America and wired for reservation on the clipper to Miami, Florida. We arrived at Port-of-Spain, Trinidad, one evening, and I sailed the next morning by clipper plane across the Carribean, eighteen hundred miles in twelve hours. By evening I was in Miami, was met by Guy Black, who was going to take part in the Mission, got his viewpoint,

12

and took the train to Chicago. I felt a little sorry that I couldn't go via New York to see the Mission secretaries there, but on arrival in Chicago I found them all in the hotel where I stopped for the night. Having settled up matters with them and started by car from Chicago to Saugatuck, I told my host, who was driving the car, of this Voice and the journey thus far. His reply was: "If you've come thus far on that certificate, then we'll get there safely and on time."

But about twenty miles from Saugatuck the hydraulic brake on the car went off, and we careened back and forth across the road, narrowly missed a ditch, and pulled up just this side of disaster. That brake had to be fixed. We went to a village five miles back to get the garage man to repair it. He worked on it for three hours, and I watched the clock. Just as we were about to cross the deadline for getting there "on time" the garage man called out, "I've got it." We jumped into the car, and just as we were driving into the camp grounds the bell was ringing for the opening of the Ashram. We were there "safely and on time"! It was twelve thousand miles of quiet miracle. I simply could not have thought out that journey beforehand, and without the assurance I would not have been able to complete the manuscript and have such a restful voyage.

But that simple incident did something else: it showed me that as God had blessed the "going out" he was blessing the "coming in," that America was to be the place of spiritual adventure as India had been, that as he had called me to India so he was calling me for the time being to America, that, as I now see, I was to walk with the Christ of the

13

American Road. The National Christian Mission was hallowed by this incident. I went through it with a deep sense of awed gratitude.

A further incident clarified and intensified this call to adventure with the Christ of the American Road. At the completion of the National Christian Mission, in which I had spoken from three to five times a day for twenty-two weeks, I was awakened one morning at four o'clock with the Inner Voice saying, "I want you here." I was startled and, quite unconvinced, reminded myself that I couldn't do it—the Mission was over, my family was in India, my work was there, the boat was to sail that day with my baggage, and I was to catch it by plane two weeks later in the Philippine Islands. Everything—passage, passport, visé—everything was arranged for me to return. But the Voice persisted, "I want you here," and after two hours of vainly struggling against it I saw that there was nothing to do but obey. I arose and wrote out five telegrams, one of which asked that my baggage be taken off the boat, as I could not go.

Perhaps I should answer the query arising in the minds of many and say that I do not habitually nor supremely rely on the "Voice" for guidance. God guides through a number of ways: supremely through the life and teaching of Jesus, through the accumulated wisdom of the Church gathered through the centuries, through personal counsel of individuals, through matching us against an open door of opportunity, through our heightened moral and spiritual intelligence, and finally through the Inner Voice. That Inner Voice usually comes only when the other ways are not relevant, or clear and decisive. But when it does come, it is self-authenticating. It does not argue with you as do the voices from the subconscious. It speaks with quiet but un-mistakable authority and assurance, and when it comes, it is always right. It has never let me down.

But what did this Voice, "I want you here," mean? What it will finally mean only the years will unfold. But it has meant, among other things, trying in a humble way over many months as a go-between to avert the war between Japan and America—"an adventure in failure." It has meant three and one-half years of painful separation from my family and from India; but it has also meant the most fruitful years of evangelism I have ever known; it has meant the writing of *Abundant Living*, which I could not have written outside of America; and above all it has meant the discovery of, and an adventure with, the Christ of the American Road.

What a Christ this is! taking the energies and pioneering spirit of a people gathered from all climes and all races, and in spite of all their sins and prejudices welding them into a living whole until they become perhaps the most united nation on earth, and perhaps the greatest.

Christ has done this? Yes, for without his spirit working at the heart of this American civilization—cleansing, inspiring, uniting—this civilization would not have been possible. He is the cement that holds it together. Through its centrifugal forces and its dividing sins it would fall to pieces tomorrow without him. He is the most cleansing, constructive, potent force working within the soul of this people—and its one hope.

A big claim? It is! But as we trace how Christ's spirit has been woven into the beginnings, the continuous history, and the future of this people, you will probably come to the conclusion that there is more there than can be told. In this book I have only glimpsed it. Someday we may grasp it, and grasp it on a wide scale, so that we may lay hold on his cleansing and regenerating power to remake and guide this dynamic entity called America.

As the dispirited disciples walked along the Emmaus Road after the crucifixion, they were joined by a stranger. Afterward, recounting what had happened, they said: "Did not our heart burn within us, while he talked with us by the way, and while he opened to us the scriptures?" It may be that as we walk down through the pages of this book we shall be joined by the Christ of the American Road; and maybe our hearts too will burn within us as he talks with us by the way, and as he opens to us the Scriptures and the covenants of our national history, and as he points us to our national destiny.

Chapter I—

WE HAVE A STARTING POINT

WE DO NOT begin with the American Road; we begin with the Christ. He was here before the American Road began and will be here after, in the centuries to come, that road may have come to its end. Twenty-two civilizations have arisen in human history, and all but seven have perished. Whether or not this one will live on will be determined by how much of the eternal we can put into its life and structure. For no greatness anywhere is proof against decay—least of all our modern precarious greatness.

No, we cannot begin with the relativisms of the American Road. We must find some starting point, some absolute, if possible, and work out from that absolute to all the relativisms of the hour.

I know that science would balk at that statement and would disclaim beginning with any absolute. We respect that attitude, and will speak of it later with deepest appreciation, and will endeavor to find a way of reconciliation. But you and I, if we are Christians, are not primarily scientists. We are primarily Christians. And a Christian is a person who has a starting point. What is that starting point, our port of departure?

Is it God? Do we start with God? Hardly. For if we start with God we really do not start with God, but with our

views of God. In the place of God we substitute a set of
views about God. That set of views becomes our God. But
the form of God may be other than our formula. Apart from
Christ we know little about God. When I see where the
speculations and guesses of men have led them in their
views of God, I become a little wary. I remarked to a priest
of a Hindu temple, pointing to some lewd frescoes of the
escapades of a Hindu god on the walls of the temple, "Can
you do these things?" To which he thoughtfully replied,
"You have to be very strong spiritually when you come to
this temple, for if you aren't you will go off and do the same
things this god does." This Hindu was better than his god.
The only hope of the worshiper was to be unlike his god.
Even the morally advanced Hebrews depicted God in ways
which now make the Christian conscience question. A mother explaining to her little girl about the murder of the
Amalekites at the command of God said that revelation was
progressive, culminating in Christ, who taught us to love
our enemies. To this the little girl replied, "Now I see; this
back here was before God was a Christian." She said something! I repeat: apart from Christ we know little about
God. We cannot, therefore, begin with God and work down
to all human problems.

Then where shall we begin? At the opposite end? With
the problems themselves? That usually ends in confusion.
If you begin with a problem, you will probably end
with a problem, and in the process you will become a
problem. Of one modern minister it was said, "Without a problem spake he not unto them." To some social
workers in a great city I remarked, "Aren't many of you
problems dealing with problems?" and the approval seemed

widespread, if not general. Two tangles don't make a solution, and if you begin with a tangle you'll end with one.

One of the outstanding Christians of this age wrote an article in a religious journal entitled "What Could a Briton Do?" The position of the writer was that being a Briton she worked out from that standpoint to the relative evils of Nazism and war. They were both evils, she said, but as she was compelled to choose between these relative evils, she chose the lesser of the two evils—reluctantly she chose war. From her starting point she was bound to come out at that place. She began with the relativism of being a Briton, worked out to the relative evils of Nazism and war, and chose the lesser of the two evils, war. But she began at the wrong place. She was not primarily a Briton. She was primarily a Christian and only secondarily a Briton. Her starting point should have been Christ. From the starting point of Christ she should have worked down to the relative evils of Nazism and war. In that case she probably would have done what I felt compelled to do: namely, reject both and choose my absolute, Christ.

For Christ is the Absolute. He is our Starting Point. He is the Master Light of all our seeing. Whatever other people do or do not do, Christians must begin with Christ, for they are Christ-ians. A Christian is one who believes in God and man and life through Christ.

We work out from Christ to God and come to our conclusions about God. And the conclusion is this: God is a Christlike God. We think that in Christ God has *shown* us what he is like. We could not have guessed it. We could never have dreamed that God was like *that!* But if he is like that which I see in Christ, he is a good God and trustable. If

19

the God that is back of the universe is like this God that I
see in Christ, then he can have my heart without qualification. For I know nothing higher for God or man than to
be Christlike. The highest adjective descriptive of character
in any language is the adjective Christlike. I can conceive of
nothing higher; I can be content with nothing less. We
believe, then, that Jesus is the human life of God; he is that
part of God we have been able to see, God speaking to us
the language of the man in the street, showing us his character where our characters are wrought out, namely, in the
stream of human history; he is the language of eternity
translated into the speech of time, the Word made flesh.

We are not primarily what the Moslems call *Ahlekitab*—
"the People of the Book"—we are primarily "the People of
the Person." It is not said in the Book, "The Word became
printer's ink," but it is said, "The Word became flesh."
Had the Word become printer's ink, we should have followed a code. Instead our code is a Character. We follow a
living mind instead of a fixed letter. Therefore our goal is
a flying goal—always ahead of us, inexhaustible. You can
exhaust a letter, you can never exhaust a Life. We value the
letters of the Book, inasmuch as the Book is the inspired
record of the Revelation, but the Revelation is in the face of
Jesus Christ. That Life was there before the letter was written, and it is in the letter and yet beyond the letter—not
different from, but beyond.

We believe that in Christ we have discovered an ultimate.
We have made progress in everything except in what constitutes goodness. There we have not progressed; we have
not even caught up. For the only argument we can find
against Christ is that he is too high, too idealistic for this

world of ours. In other words, we confess he is still ahead of us. The highest compliment that can be paid to any man, or to God for that matter, is to say he is Christlike. A man lived among us for three years, and you can transfer every quality of character from him to God without lowering your estimate of God. Lowering? You heighten your ideas of God when you think of him in terms of Christ.

Three swift years—and in those three swift years we saw the meaning of eternity. Impossible to reveal the character of the illimitable and timeless God in so short a time? The nature of a character can be seen in a flash—the revelation of a moment. One of the members of our Ashram said: "I see little of my roommate, for when I'm in the room he's out, and when I'm out he's in, but I think I know my roommate. I woke up one morning and found my shoes blacked. I saw him in that thoughtful deed." We see God in this deed —this deed called Christ. Just as through the chinks of a fence you can see a vast panorama, so through the chinks of the life of Christ we can see the vast panorama of eternity. And as we gaze we are awed at the sight of the redemptive God. Awed? We instinctively kneel in humble adoration, forever captured by that kind of God. The God of the nail-pierced hands has me—forever!

We believe that in Jesus Christ we have an ultimate. Does that stop progress? It begins it! You cannot make progress until you get something fixed. In mathematics as long as you are not sure whether two and two make four, six, or ten you cannot go on. "Two and two make four" is an ultimate. We have not been able, and we shall not be able, to improve on that. Does the discovery of this ultimate stop mathematical progress? It begins it. For on this fixed ultimate you can build up vast mathematical calculations. The perfect becomes the progressive. In geometry "things equal to the same thing are equal to each other." That is fixed. But upon that fixed axiom you build vast geometrical calculations. Again the perfect becomes the progressive. We are adding no new notes to the musical scale. Does that stop musical progress? Within the fixed scale vast symphonies have been born and new ones will be born.

In Jesus Christ we believe that we have struck a moral and spiritual ultimate. The moral and spiritual universe is in epitome in him; he is the revelation of its nature. Now we know what God is, and what man may become. We know where we ought to head in. Mankind need no longer drift on troubled waters without chart or compass or star. We have all three. Beyond that which is found in Christ the human race will not progress. He is a moral ultimate.

Does that stop progress? It begins it. For while Christ is behind us in history—the pattern, the norm—nevertheless he is beyond us, ahead of us, on the further side of our twenty centuries. If he is God's final revelation, he is also God's unfolding revelation. He provided for an unfolding revelation of himself: "I have yet many things to say unto you, but ye cannot bear them now. Howbeit when he, the Spirit of Truth, is come, he will guide you into all truth: . . . for he shall receive of mine, and shall show it unto you." The things which the Spirit of Truth shows are not different from, but are more than, the things Jesus was able to disclose when here in bodily form. If the revelation had been in the letter we should have outgrown it, but since it is in a life we shall never outgrow it. For we are forever catching new meanings and finding more and more applications of the principle of this inexhaustible life. He is a flying goal, forever ahead of us. And yet he is realizable. For since he is the revealer of the nature of reality, we can embody that reality to the extent of our capacity. Note "to the extent of our capacity"; not to the extent of his capacity—that is limitless. We have him, and yet we haven't him. He is so near, so tenderly near, and yet so remote. He satisfies us to the depths of our beings, and yet in that very act he stirs us to deeper unsatisfactions for more and yet more. The more I see in him the more I see there is to be seen. I see, and yet I am almost blinded by what there is to be seen.

We, as Christians, have a starting point—Christ. Christianity is Christ. To be a Christian is to respond to all the meanings you find in Christ. If that is so, then we are forever under the law of growth. The finite will forever approach the Infinite, and find in that growth its eternal happiness.

As I have sat in Round Table conferences and have listened to men of all faiths, and of no faith, talking about their way of life, and revealing their confusions, I have almost involuntarily clutched an invisible something in my hand. I have whispered to my inmost self, "You've got the key." I have. That key—Christ.

When you don't begin with him, life's sums won't add up. When you do begin with him, life's sums do add up. Start at some other place and you go from tangle to tangle, from snarl to snarl. The head of one of the Japanese Relocation Centers said to me: "In these camps there is a basically wrong starting point: American citizens are here without just cause. That basic wrong sets everything awry. No valid motives can be appealed to, so nothing comes out right." You must get your starting point right. The universe will not back any starting except that which starts with Christ. Then and only then will your sums come out right.

That is the basic trouble with the world today. We begin at the wrong place, and so we end at the wrong place. A French writer says: "Everything happens today as if thought were out of gear, as if the wheel were no longer in line with the motor. . . . I believe that when things go wrong in the material world it must always be due to some original spiritual error." The original spiritual error is not to begin with Christ, and not to follow through with him. If you do not, then your universe will tumble to pieces. Life won't back it.

An Episcopal bishop told me that something I had written cured him of what he called "a mild species of episcopal swearing": "Formerly when I went along the roads at night I dimmed my lights at the approach of a car. If the other man responded and dimmed his lights, then well and good; but if he didn't, then when we got near I flashed my lights up into his face to show him what I thought of him. Now," he said, "I see that I must not allow the other man to determine my conduct. I must work out from my own principles to every situation. So now when I approach another car I dim my lights. If the other man responds, well and good; but if he doesn't, I keep mine dimmed. I find it safer, and moreover I feel more like a bishop!" In the first instance he began at the other man's action and worked back to his own. Result? Disgruntled and out of sorts. The universe was against him. In the second he began at Christ and continued through no matter what the other man did. The universe approved; he inwardly felt at home with reality.

We Have a Starting Point

A group of prominent Christians opposed the feeding of the starving of Europe·on the ground of expediency. Then they changed and advocated the feeding, again on the ground of expediency. In a long, labored statement they told why they had now come to this conclusion. Not one was a Christian reason. It was all on the basis of relative expediency. One would have thought that Christians would have said something like this: "Christians, according to their Master, if possible feed everybody in need, friend and enemy alike. Our friends are starving in Europe; we, as Christians, can and must feed them." That would have been simple and Christian. The other was complicated and pagan.

In the Washington Cathedral a minister arose in a ministers' meeting and said: "Don't we have to act on expediencies? For instance, Caiaphas said, 'It is expedient for us that one man die for the people, and that the whole nation perish not.'" I reminded my questioner that this gospel of expediency is the gospel according to Caiaphas, and not the gospel according to Christ. Moreover, the gospel Caiaphas preached was the devil's atonement; he was planning somebody else's sacrifice to save the nation. When you plan somebody else's sacrifice, and not your own, that is the devil's atonement. Christ planned his own sacrifice to save the nation. That is Christ's atonement. Do you preach the gospel according to Caiaphas or according to Christ? It matters much in the outcome whether you begin with Caiaphas or with Christ.

Here at the nation's capital was a Christian minister stationed there to give moral and spiritual guidance to a nation in a crisis, and he preached the gospel of Caiaphas! It was an easy gospel to preach, for it was the nation's mood; the

25

older generation, most of whom would not go to war, was planning the sacrifices of the younger generation. It was expedient, they said. It was all dangerously near the gospel of Caiaphas.

The expediency of Caiaphas ended long ago in the crucifixion of Christ. If you begin with anything other than Christ, you end in crucifying him and others—and incidentally yourself. A wrong starting point—confusion, complexity, crucifixion. A right starting point—clarity, conviction, consummation.

This age is coming out wrong because it is starting wrong. Aldous Huxley said in a reflective mood: "The bitter fruit of the tree of philosophy made me re-examine its roots." He found that the roots of the tree of modern philosophy were not grounded in Christ, hence its bitter fruit. He changed. And he changed to Christ.

The starting point for the Christian is Christ!

Chapter II—

TWO LINES CONVERGE IN HISTORY

THERE ARE TWO great streams of human longings which have run through human history: a longing for a new order, and a longing for a leader.

History is His Story—the story of God awakening within man twin desires: the desire for a new order of justice and harmony, and the desire for a leader who will lead man into that order. These two desires seem universal.

First the desire for a new order. We are not at home in this one. We live within it only under protest. Dr. Frederick W. Norwood expressed this dissatisfaction in the words: "Whenever the spirit of Christ is strong within me, I feel a foreigner to a thousand customs in my country." We all do. But this is not confined to Christians. Evidently the "Light which lighteth every man that cometh into the world" makes man feel a divine discontent with things as they are. The "ought-to-be" stands over against the "is" and disturbs and calls it.

"The next station is Ur of the Chaldees," called out the railway conductor or guard on the train through Mesopotamia. As we stepped out and looked at the vast desert ruins an Englishman remarked: "So this is the place Abraham got out of. No wonder!" But when Abraham left it to go out "not knowing whither he went," this Ur was the seat of one of the mightiest empires of history. Yet the divine discontent in Abraham said: "This city has no foundations; it is founded on blood and fear and exploiting injustice; it will crumble. I will seek a city of God—a city which has foundations." ("For he looked for a city which hath foundations"—Heb. 11:10.) From that day to this, man has been seeking that city, that order which has foundations; for he has felt that the order in which he lives, with its injustices and inequalities, is crumbling under his feet—it is without foundations.

So men have dreamed and planned for a new order. Plato with his Republic; the Hindus with their *Satya Yug,* the Age of Truth; Moore with his Utopia; Bellamy "Looking Backward"; H. G. Wells dreaming of "The Shape of Things to Come"; Mahatma Gandhi with his *Rama Rajya,* the Kingdom of Rama; the Hebrew prophets who looked and longed for the new order when men should beat their swords into plowshares, when righteousness should cover the earth as the waters cover the sea—all these were under the divine discontent and call. And now the longing has become epidemic. What was the lone vision of a few prophets and seers has become the growing passion of the whole human race. Never before in human history have so many thought and planned for world reconstruction. In churches, in clubs, in schools and colleges, in trains and barber shops, in convention halls, in legislative councils, and in the silences of the individual heart, the longing for a new order clamors for expression—usually with a sigh and a fear lest man be not sufficiently enlightened or strong enough to bring that order into being. If man doesn't get his new order he will die of homesickness. The natives of Tasmania were taken from that land and removed to another island to make room for the white man's pushing civilization. They literally died of homesickness. They would stand upon the cliffs looking toward their beloved land and with tears streaming down their cheeks cry: "My land, my land!" Apart from their land they withered and literally perished as a race. We today feel that mankind will perish through sheer homesickness and through mutual strife unless he can get to his real order, the order for which he is made, for he feels this old order going to pieces beneath his feet. So widespread and deep has this longing become that maybe, at last, man is in the beginnings of seeing the fruit of his soul's desire. Unabashed and unbroken by disappointment he hopes on, knowing that "whatever ought to be will be, God being God." And he knows that this new order *ought* to be.

But that longing for a new order is accompanied by another longing—the longing for a leader. This leader will lead into that new order, but will also embody in himself the new order. He will be the new order personalized. This longing too is widespread. The Hindus long for the coming of the *Niskalank Avatar*—the "Spotless Incarnation" who will usher in the Age of Truth, the *Satya Yug*. The Mexican Aztecs believed that Quetzalcoatl, the legendary righteous king who went away toward the east, would return to deliver them. And so when the Spanish Cortez came they thought he might be their king-deliverer. But alas, like many another longing for a deliverer, their hopes were dashed, for Cortez was rapacious rather than redemptive. The Hebrews too believed that their Messiah

29

would come, and his coming would mean their deliverance and the beginning of the new day.

In our present world the "leadership principle" has come to the surface in Nazism and Fascism. Why? The reason seems to be that men are made for loyalty to a leader—a leader who embodies a cause. We shall see that men are also made for freedom, but freedom to follow an ideal embodied in a leader. In a land where the impersonal is supposed to be the highest category of being, Tulsi Das, a great poet of India, said, "The Impersonal laid no hold on my heart." Impersonal causes and ideals leave men comparatively cold. Only when those causes and ideals become embodied in a person do they lay hold of the hearts of men and shake them like a passion. Loyalty to a person is one of the strongest attachments of the human race.

Here, then, are two lines of longing running through human history—a longing for a new order and a longing for a leader. Again and again both desires have been mocked as dreams of a new order have faded and leaders have let their followers down. It is a sad story of disappointment and disillusionment. And yet—and yet men have hoped on and prayed on, feeling that the real cause and the real person would come.

They have come! These two lines in history converged and met in a man—the Man of Nazareth. In him the longing for an order and the longing for a person coincide and are one. The desires of the ages met in him. The Kingdom of God is the Order, and he himself is the Person.

The fact of the order and the person coinciding in Christ is perhaps the most important thing in the Gospels—and the most overlooked! As this order-person was being unfolded in a recent group a prominent churchman said, "All my life I've studied theology and attended conferences, and yet I've never seen it before. I have missed perhaps the most important thing in the Gospels." He had.

Is this fact of Christ embodying an order something imposed by later thought, or is it part of the warp and woof of the very Gospels themselves? It is a part of them. It is not found here and there in an isolated text; rather it is in the very texture of the whole. It could not be clearly seen until the molds of our individualistic thinking had been broken by the rise of totalitarianisms. At first we Christians, with our interpretations of the Gospels arising out of individualism, were frightened. It was all so new and strange. We were driven back to our Bibles, and there, to our astonishment, we discovered that we have a totalitarianism that is complete. The totalitarianism is this: we are to seek first, last, and always the Kingdom of God, and this in every portion of our beings, in every relationship of life. This supreme dominance reaches into the inmost thought, and controls and redeems it, and then reaches out to the outermost relationship and also controls and redeems that. Nothing—absolutely nothing in heaven or on earth—is to be outside of its purview, its control, and its redemption.

This absolute Order brings life under a single unity, breaking down all compartmentalisms and all dualisms. It brings what all life needs: a center of authority and unity. For in our inmost beings we are made, first and foremost, for obedience. Only secondarily are we made for freedom. A sign in a chain drugstore says: "He

31

who seeks something greater than freedom will lose both the freedom and the thing itself." This is profoundly wrong. We have made freedom first in modern life, and the result is that we have lost that freedom. For freedom is a by-product of a great obedience. Sacred Writ does not say, "Seek ye first freedom," but, "Seek ye first the Kingdom of God, . . . and all these things," including freedom, "will be added unto you." For, as we shall see, in obeying the Kingdom of God we obey the very laws of our own being; hence we find our own freedom. We obey that for which we are made.

This absolute Order breaks down the dualisms between heaven and earth, between secular and sacred, the material and the spiritual, the personal and the social, and gives life a central unity. When we rediscover this Order, it will make the lesser pseudo-totalitarianisms look sick and anemic. They are not total enough! They are only half-gods. We want a real God whom we can completely obey and in whose obedience we shall find perfect freedom. Jesus went out proclaiming that absolute Order, and then to our astonishment identified himself with that absolute Order. To the tracing of this identification, and to the implications of that identification for religion and life, we now turn.

We have seen the two lines of longing for an order and for a person. Jesus saw that the Kingdom of God, God's Order, fulfills the longing for an order, and he himself fulfills the longing for a person. And in the end he wove them into one. He said: "From the days of John the Baptist till now the Realm of heaven [or, the Kingdom of Heaven—A.V.] suffers violence, and the violent press into it. For all the prophets and the Law prophesied of it [the Kingdom] until John."

(Matt. 11:12-13—Moffatt, 1st ed.) "All the prophets and the Law prophesied of it": they stood on tiptoe looking for this new Order, but now the prophecy is fact—the Kingdom is here, and "he that is least in the Kingdom of Heaven is greater than he [John the Baptist]." Jesus further said this Kingdom is fulfillment: "I will not any more eat thereof, until it be fulfilled in the Kingdom of God." What was this Passover which he was eating with them, and how is it "fulfilled" in the Kingdom of God? The Passover feast commemorated the passing of the Hebrews from Egyptian bondage to the Promised Land. The Kingdom "fulfills" the longings of men to pass from the bondage of the present order to the Promised Land, the Homeland of the Soul, the Kingdom of God. He proclaimed the Kingdom as fulfillment.

But he also proclaimed himself as fulfillment: "I am not come to destroy, but to fulfill." (Matt. 5:17.) This is a generic statement, locally applied to the law and the prophets, but capable of a wider application. He fulfills that almost universal longing for a leader-savior. He proclaimed the Kingdom as fulfillment, and he proclaimed himself as fulfillment. He and the Kingdom are one!

John the Baptist took up the note of the Kingdom and cried: "Repent ye: for the Kingdom of Heaven is at hand. . . . Prepare ye the way of the Lord, make his paths straight." (Matt. 3:2-3.) He announced the Kingdom, and ended by saying, "Prepare the way of the *Lord*." The coming of the Kingdom and the coming of the Lord are one. To repent for the sake of the Kingdom and to prepare the way of the Lord are one and the same thing. The Order and the Person are inseparable.

Take another passage: "Blessed are they which are persecuted for righteousness' sake: for theirs is the Kingdom of Heaven. Blessed are ye, when men . . . shall say all manner of evil against you falsely, for my sake." (Matt. 5:10-11.) Here Jesus used interchangeably the phrases "for righteousness' sake" and "for my sake"—an amazing assumption that he is identified with "righteousness"! In case you are persecuted "for righteousness' sake" or "for my sake" you get the Kingdom of Heaven. "For I am that Kingdom of Heaven," he was saying.

"Not everyone that saith unto me, Lord, Lord, shall enter into the Kingdom of Heaven" (Matt. 7:21), the assumption being that if you really do call me "Lord" and mean it, then you do enter the Kingdom of Heaven. The relationship with him determines the relationship to the Kingdom of Heaven.

"And another also said, Lord, I will follow thee; but let me first go bid them farewell which are at home at my house. And Jesus said unto him, No man, having put his hand to the plow, and looking back, is fit for the Kingdom of God." (Luke 9:61-62.) The first verse speaks of following Jesus—"I will follow thee"—and the second of being "fit for the Kingdom of God." In other words, your attitude in following Jesus determines your fitness for the Kingdom of God. They are one.

"Well then, every scribe who has become a disciple of the Realm of heaven [the Kingdom of God] is like a householder who produces what is new and what is old from his stores." (Matt. 13:52—Moffatt.) Here men are to be "disciples of the Realm of heaven," and in another place he said, "If any man would be my disciple." In other words we

34

are to be disciples of the Order—the Kingdom of God—and disciples of the Person—Christ.

Incidentally it may be remarked that it is interesting that Jesus said that a "scribe" should bring forth something "new." A scribe was a dry-as-dust copyist; he created nothing. But, said Jesus, if you become a disciple of this new Order, though you have been as dry as a scribe, you will bring forth the new. Religion, now as dry and musty as a scribe, will become creative and dynamic and popping with newness if it really gets hold of the Kingdom—or better, if the Kingdom gets hold of it! All the dry platitudes, unrelated to life, will suddenly take on new meaning and universal relevancy.

Again, Jesus said: "Suffer little children, and forbid them not, to come unto me; for of such is the Kingdom of Heaven." (Matt. 19:14.) Here "to come unto me" and to be of the Kingdom of Heaven are synonymous. They are one. In that same chapter Jesus said to the rich young ruler: "Go and sell that thou hast, . . . and come and follow me. . . . He went away sorrowful: for he had great possessions. Then said Jesus unto his disciples, . . . A rich man shall hardly enter into the Kingdom of Heaven. . . . It is easier for a camel to go through the eye of a needle, than for a rich man to enter into the Kingdom of God." (Matt. 19: 21-24.) Here to "follow me" and to "enter into the Kingdom of God" are one; they are inextricably bound up together. Incidentally, the Kingdom of Heaven and the Kingdom of God are used interchangeably in this passage. They are the same.

Elsewhere we read: "If your foot is a hindrance to you, cut it off: better get into Life a cripple. . . . If your eye is

35

a hindrance to you, tear it out: better get into God's Realm with one eye. . . ." (Mark 9:45-47—Moffatt.) Here getting into "Life" and getting into God's Realm or Kingdom are used interchangeably. Then the Kingdom of God is "Life"! But Jesus said, "I am . . . the Life." Then both Jesus and the Kingdom are "Life"!

When Jesus was coming into Jerusalem in the triumphal entry, the disciples shouted, "Blessed be he who comes in the Lord's name! Blessed be the Reign [or Kingdom] to come, our Father David's reign!" (Mark 11:9-10—Moffatt.) Note "Blessed be *he* who comes" and "Blessed be the *Reign* to come." The coming of the Person and the coming of the Kingdom are the same. It may be noted, incidentally, that the disciples took this universal Kingdom and made it identical with "our Father David's reign." It was too big for their small hearts, so they tried to jam it into a nationalistic mold. They didn't reject it; they reduced it. We do the same; we make the Kingdom of God into "the Kingdom of our father Wesley," "the Kingdom of our father Calvin." We too reduce it!

Again: " 'The Reign of God is not coming as you hope to catch sight of it; no one will say, "Here it is" or "There it is." ' . . . To his disciples he said, 'There will come days when you will long and long in vain to have even one day of the Son of man. Men will say, "See, here he is!" "See, there he is!" but never go to them.' " (Luke 17:20-23—Moffatt.) He bound up together, "There *it* is" (vs. 21), the Kingdom, and, "there *he* is" (vs. 23), the Person.

When Peter said, "Lo, we have left all, and followed thee," Jesus replied, "Verily I say unto you, There is no man that hath left house, or parents, or brethren, or wife, or children, for the Kingdom of God's sake. . . ." (Luke 18: 28, 29.) Jesus bound up leaving all to follow him with leaving all for the Kingdom's sake. "For my sake" and "for the Kingdom of God's sake" are the same.

We must now note that Jesus did an astonishing thing when, after going out and announcing "the Kingdom of *God*," he ended up by making that Kingdom *his own*. "That ye may eat and drink at my table in my Kingdom." (Luke 22:30.) Note the "my Kingdom," not "God's Kingdom." Again, when he stood before Pilate he said, "*My* Kingdom." (John 18:36.) Again: "The Son of man shall send forth his angels, and they shall gather out of his Kingdom all things that offend." (Matt. 13:41.) Note "*his* Kingdom," and yet (vs. 43) it is "the Kingdom of their Father." As he identified himself with the Father, so he identified himself with the Father's Kingdom.

One more reference before we close this brief study of the Gospel passages. When Peter made the great confession, "Thou art the Christ, the Son of the living God," Jesus replied, "Blessed art thou, Simon Bar-jona: for flesh and blood hath not revealed it unto thee, but my Father which is in heaven. . . . I will give unto thee the keys of the Kingdom of Heaven: and whatsoever thou shalt bind on earth shall be bound in heaven." (Matt. 16:16-19.) What are "the keys of the Kingdom of Heaven" given to Peter? Does he stand at the gate of heaven with a bunch of keys to let people in, or keep them out, as current crude conceptions imply? I hope not. No man is good enough or wise enough for that task. Only God could decide that. Then what are the keys? The context tells us. Peter, through the revelation of the Father given to him, had grasped who Jesus was: "Thou art the Christ, the Son of the living God." Jesus replied, "Peter, you have the keys to the Kingdom. You know who I am; now you know what the Kingdom is. The key to my nature is the key to the nature of the Kingdom. I am the revelation of the nature of God, and I am the revelation of the nature of God's Reign. You have the Key. And this is valid in heaven and on earth. What you bind on earth is bound in heaven. The nature of the Reign of God in heaven and the nature of the Reign of God on earth are the same. The moral universe is one. This Reign is one—in heaven and on earth. And I am the Key."

If the objection is raised that Jesus said "keys" and not "key," then perhaps we may note that a master key is a key made up of all keys. Christ is that Master Key that unlocks everything in heaven and on earth. If you know Christ, you know the Kingdom, for the Kingdom is Christ-likeness universalized.

If there are those who feel that though the Gospels bind up Jesus and the Kingdom, nevertheless the disciples, particularly Paul, put asunder what God had joined together, emphasizing the Person and dropping out the Order, then let us look for clarification of this point in a few final passages. After the Resurrection Jesus talked with his disciples for forty days about "the things pertaining to the Kingdom of God." (Acts 1:3.) His last emphasis would be upon the new Order of God. He knew the danger of their being attached to his Person, leaving out the Order. If they did this it would change the very nature of the redemptive movement he was launching. Seeing his emphasis on the Kingdom, his disciples inquired: "Lord, wilt thou at this time restore the kingdom to Israel?" (Vs. 6.) They thought the Kingdom would be attached to Israel. "You're wrong," he said. "The Kingdom is going to be attached to me, and not to Israel. . . . Ye shall be witnesses unto me, both in Jerusalem, and in all Judea, and in Samaria, and unto the uttermost part of the earth." (Vs. 8.) You are to witness universally to a universal Kingdom embodied in a universal Person.

When we go on in the Acts we find this same emphasis continued. We read: "They believed Philip, who preached the gospel of the Reign of God and the name of Jesus." (Acts 8:12—Moffatt.) It was a double gospel, and yet one —the gospel of the Kingdom of God and the name of Jesus. The Order and the Person are the two sides of the one gospel. Later we read: "To whom he expounded and testified the Kingdom of God, persuading them concerning Jesus." (Acts 28:23.) Paul "expounded"—the Kingdom is something to be understood. He "testified"—it is something to be experienced. But above all the Kingdom is embodied in a Person: "persuading them concerning Jesus."

The Acts ends in these words: "Paul dwelt two whole years in his own hired house, and received all that came in unto him, preaching the Kingdom of God, and teaching those things which concern the Lord Jesus Christ." (Acts 28:30-31.) Note "preaching the Kingdom of God, and teaching . . . the Lord Jesus Christ." The curtain falls with those two things—the Kingdom and the Person—together in the message of Christianity's chief exponent, Paul.

Later the Church separated them and preached the Person without the Order. By the time the creeds were written the Kingdom had dropped out, or was pushed into a heavenly world. It was not an operating force now. The Apostles', the Athanasian, and the Nicean Creeds—the creeds which sum up the teaching of the early Church—mention once, and only once, the Kingdom of God, and that beyond the borders of this life—a heavenly Kingdom: "Thy Kingdom is an everlasting Kingdom." Jesus used "the Kingdom of God," or its equivalent, a hundred times. The creeds used it once. The creeds concentrated on interpreting this personal Christ. They did not expound what he expounded. A note—the keynote—had been dropped out. The nature of Christianity was changed—it was a personal relationship with a Person-Saviour. With the Order gone it lacked social meanings for the total life. A crippled Christianity went across Europe, leaving a crippled result. The Christianity we have inherited from Europe isn't big enough to meet the demands of this hour of breakdown and reconstruction. It has exhausted itself against the problems of this hour.

There is one hope—the hope of rediscovering and re-applying the original Christianity of Christ, for in him the Order and the Person are inextricably one. What does the binding together of these two mean for religion? It means that religion is intensely personal, for it is a personal relationship with a Person. To preach the Kingdom of God without the Person makes our religion a loyalty to an impersonal Order. That lacks depth of personal meaning. You can be loyal to an order, but you cannot love it. Moreover you get tired of an impersonal idea. You can get sick of the abstract idea of "Beauty," but when beauty meets you in a person then beauty is compelling, warming, and you are almost irresistibly drawn. The gospel of the Kingdom of God preached alone without the Person is interesting and arouses loyalty, but it lacks the tender intimacies of a personal relationship to a person. That is one reason why the gospel of the Kingdom of God as preached in America a generation ago exhausted itself and degenerated into social service. It lacked being embodied in a Person.

On the other hand, to preach the Person without the Kingdom makes religion degenerate into a private affair between you and your personal Saviour. It lacks social conscience and social redemption. It isn't relevant for all of life. But if you put them together, then your religion is at once personal and social. Not now personal and now social, but personal and social by the very nature of the relationship. For if you have personal relationships with a Person who embodies an Order, then you must have relationships with everything with which that Order has relationships. But that Order is completely totalitarian; it has relationships with everything. Therefore your religion has relationships with everything. Nothing is alien from its purview and its redemption. All life—personal and collective—must bend the knee, submit, and surrender to this absolute Order, to find itself again. Therefore I am not interested in a "personal gospel" or a "social gospel." I want one gospel—a gospel which lays its hand on all life, personal and social, and controls and redeems it.

What is it that makes Mahatma Gandhi so significant? As a man he is very insignificant—large ears, teeth gone in front, scrawny. Then why his significance? The reason is that he embodies a cause. When he speaks, the cause of India's freedom speaks. Therefore the people hang upon his words as upon an oracle. To be loyal to Gandhi is to be loyal to the cause. Gandhi as a person has significance beyond himself—the significance of the cause.

Why is it that Abraham Lincoln is increasingly the greatest American produced by our civilization? Because we feel that in Lincoln the cause of democracy has come to embodiment—a democracy for white and black, for everybody. Democracy looks out of his sad eyes and touches us with great rugged hands. Democracy meets us in a person. So democracy becomes power.

If Jesus Christ were only a Person I would follow him to the death. But I would instinctively know there was something lacking. He would lack social and corporate significance. He would be a personal way to a personal deliverance, which is good, but is not good enough. For life demands total reconstruction. Evil can be in the individual will; it can be in the corporate will. There is such a thing as an evil soul; there is such a thing as an evil system. The total life must be totally reconstructed. Can Christ be a Saviour *there?* Not if he is just a Person. But if he is a Person embodying an Order? And not only that, but an absolute Person embodying an absolute Order? That is different—and decisive.

Christ is just that. He is the absolute Order personalized. In him the government of God, which stretches from the lowest cell to the farthermost star and includes everything between, comes to embodiment. The Kingdom of God in him looks out at us with tender eyes, touches us with warm, redemptive hands, and hence shakes us like a passion. Absolute authority and absolute love meet us in him. He rules and he redeems.

In one of my books I refer to being shaken by my visit to

Russia, for there I saw great things being done for the underprivileged, but being done in the name of atheism. I needed reassurance. One morning in Moscow that assurance came; there arose out of the pages of Scripture a verse, authoritative, speaking directly to my inmost being: "Receiving a kingdom which cannot be shaken." (Heb. 12:28—Weymouth.) An unshakable Kingdom! In the midst of kingdoms shaken to their depths and crumbling to ruin through their own contradictions and sins, here was a Kingdom unshaken. The Kingdom of God is not shaken; it stands the one solid reality amid a shaken and a shakable world. I breathed deeply with a sense of glorious satisfaction. And yet I was not satisfied; so I went back again the next morning. This time another verse arose and spoke to my condition: "Jesus Christ the same yesterday, and today, and forever." (Heb. 13:8.) An unchanging Person! In the midst of a changing world he stands unchanged. Two things were in my mind and heart: an unshakable Kingdom and an unchanging Person. I rejoiced in them. But they were apart—they were two things, not one. Now they are one. The unshakable Kingdom meets me in the unchanging Person. Now I do not merely rejoice; I bend the knee in unspeakable awe that at last we have the answer. That answer is not Christ, as we often say; that answer is Christ the Person embodying the Order, the Kingdom. If that isn't the answer, then there is none. But everything within me says it is the answer! "It is God's answer that will answer to the Pharaoh," said Joseph. (Gen. 41:16—Moffatt.) And today it is God's answer, and only God's answer, which will answer to the world. The half-answers are breaking down, going down in fire and ruin. Only God's answer will stand up to the world need.

There is another implication of real importance if Christ embodies the Kingdom. He is not only the revelation of the nature of God but also the revelation of the nature of God's reign. If God *redeems* in terms of Christ, he also *rules* in terms of Christ. He does not redeem in terms of Christ and rule in other terms. He redeems by a cross, and he rules by a cross. There is a false distinction made when we say God redeems by a cross but rules by a throne and that the cross and the throne are different. That introduces into the nature of God a dualism, and there cannot be one. The cross and the throne are one. When Jesus had decided upon the cross as the way out, he then added: "Now is this world to be judged"—the cross was to be the judgment throne; "now shall the Prince of this world be expelled"—evil powers will be expelled by a cross. "But I, when I am lifted up from the earth [on the cross], will draw all men unto myself" (John 12:31-33—Moffatt) —the final power over men was the power of the cross. Here the cross and the throne coincide and are one. This means that the Kingdom will be brought in by no means other than Christlike means. If the Kingdom were brought in by means other than Christlike means, then it wouldn't be the Kingdom—it would be something else. Its very nature would change by the nature of the means used to bring it in. For "the means pre-exist in and determine the ends." We must sweep away from our thinking and acting and planning the idea that we can bring in the Kingdom of God by wrong means, dismissing the means when we get to the end. For the means pass on into the ends—inevitably. Therefore Jesus, on the very threshold

44

of the announcing of the gospel of the Kingdom, rejected, in the wilderness temptations, all means for bringing in that Kingdom inconsistent with the nature of that Kingdom. The prevalent and disastrous idea that "the end justifies the means" was swept from the board.

The absolute Order confronts us in the absolute Person, but that Order can be brought into being only by means consistent with the spirit of that Person.

Here, then, in this Person converge the two streams of longing running through history—the longing for an order and the longing for a leader. Men have looked to local leaders representing local causes—a Hitler representing the cause of the superior race, a Mussolini representing the cause of the superior state, a Lenin representing the cause of the superior class, the class of the proletariat. These half-leaders with half-causes have let men down, or will let men down, for the universe in the end won't back their ways. They and their causes break down. They and their causes will continue to arise and decay until we turn to the Person and the Order whom the universe will back. "I lay all in ruins, ruins, ruins; everything shall be overturned, till the rightful man arrives—and I will give him everything." (Ezek. 21:27—Moffatt.) The judgments of God are laying all in ruins, ruins, ruins, and everything is being and shall be overturned—the universe guarantees the instability of evil—until the Rightful Man arrives. Who is this Rightful Man to whom everything shall be given? Who, except Christ?

Charles Lamb once said, "If Shakespeare should come into this room we would all rise; but if Jesus Christ should come in we would all kneel!" Why? Do men feel instinctively that he is the Rightful Man?

A man was addressing a group of hardened laborers who kept their hats on and smoked while he talked. In the midst of the address the speaker said, "Jesus Christ is coming in at that door." Instantly every cap went off and every cigarette and every pipe was put away as they turned to the door to look. Why this instinctive reverence? Is he the Rightful Man to whom everything shall be given? Will everything be given to him because everything is made to work in his way and in no other way? Are all things, all men, made by him, and will they refuse ultimately to obey until they hear their Master's voice? "Without him was not anything made that was made." If the touch of Christ is upon the structure of all things, animate and inanimate, then by their very nature they cannot live in any way except his way. When they try to work some other way they work their own ruin—as now. Things and persons will find their way to harmony in him and in him alone.

For there is only one universal Man and only one universal Order. Buddha was Indian, Confucius was Chinese, Moses was Hebrew, Socrates was Greek, Shakespeare was English, Goethe was German, Garibaldi was Italian, Lincoln an American—all were local. Only one transcended the boundaries of race and class and country—only one was the Son of Man. Not the Son of the East nor the Son of the West, but the Son of Man—of man as man. The Nordic depicts him with blue eyes and blonde hair; the Hindu depicts him with brown skin and seated in deep realization; the African depicts him with thick lips and black skin; the Chinese with yellow skin and slant eyes—why? He seems to belong to everybody. Everybody is at home in his company—everybody except the evil, and they too are drawn by a goodness that attracts and redeems, rather than one that judges and repels.

Moreover, he is the only one who transcends sex. For in him is the tenderness of the woman and the strength and courage of the man. So both men and women see fulfilled in him their own finest selves. Again, he is the only one who thought in terms of a world Kingdom and in terms of little children. Children, unafraid of the Ruler of all, climb into his lap, stroke his face with chubby hands, and say by their acts: "This is the Rightful Man." Laborers grasp the hardened hand of a fellow Laborer, a Carpenter, and know that he understands, that he is the Rightful Man. Men of large affairs know that when they look into those eyes— eyes that have a world dominion in them—they have met their Master, and that they who have been used to giving orders must now obey. They know that this is the Rightful Man. The learned know that in him language was reduced from verbal complexity to fact, and that his learning was a life—a life that knew all things. And the ignorant know that he has brought learning from the high shelves of pedantry and placed it on the table where the simple can taste and be fed. And rulers know that their rule is based on sand unless it is based on his way, that he is the rightful Ruler—the Rightful Man. And soldiers know, as the centurion did, that he could meet death without a friend, without a drug, and yet could be masterful even in torture's grasp. And the sinful, stricken with pangs of conscience, know that in him stands what they ought to be and, greater still, what they can be by his grace. He and he **alone** is the Rightful Man.

And there is only one universal Order. Plato's Republic was Grecian; Mahatma Gandhi's *Rama Rajya* is Indian and Hindu; Japan's "new order for Asia" is Japanese; Fascism, Nazism, and Communism are European; the British Commonwealth is British; the "American century" is American. All the plans of men for reconstruction are just themselves written large and projected on the screen of world affairs— they triumph through the triumph of their ideas. Only one plan gathers up all the good of the lesser plans and eliminates their wrongs; only one plan can appeal to all men, of all races; and that plan is God's plan—the Kingdom of God.

You say, "Men will not take it"? They will have to, or perish. For life will not work in any other way. So if intelligent choice will not lead man to Christ, then sorrow and frustration and disillusionment may yet "toss him to my breast." Perhaps men on a large scale will get tired of "ruins, ruins, ruins," and everything being "overturned," and be driven by sheer necessity to accept and follow the Rightful Man, Christ, and the Rightful Order, his Order.

We have arrived, then, at a supreme value. Paul speaks of "the supreme value of knowing Christ Jesus my Lord" —the Leader. (Phil. 3:8—Moffatt.) And Jesus said, "Seek ye first the Kingdom of God"—the Order. We are to hold as "supreme value," and to "seek first" the Person-Order, and the pledge is that "all these things"—everything we need—shall be added. Hold something else as supreme value and seek something else first, and all these things shall be subtracted from you—as now!

Here, then, is our Frame of Reference, our Final Word, our Point of Departure, the Master Light of all our seeing, our Absolute. We can now work down from this Absolute to the relativisms of the American Road. Having looked at the Christ we may now look at the Christ of the American Road.

Chapter III—

WHAT AND WHERE IS AMERICA?

Now THAT WE have established a viewpoint we can look at this tremendous entity called America—tremendous in its possibilities for good or ill. I think I can understand the feeling of the Chinese Christian girl who on the eve of landing in America spent the night in prayer to be made worthy to land on and live in a Christian land. She was doomed to many a disillusionment, for ours is not yet a Christian land. Christ has penetrated deeply into our land, and the best things have his hallmark upon them, but there are vast areas of our individual and collective life still pagan. Nevertheless the Chinese girl was right. I feel that same sense of awe as my ship of thought sails through the Golden Gate to land on and explore this pulsating fact called America. What is America?

A Hindu pundit, learned in ancient lore, so much so that he had cut himself off from modern learning, called on an English missionary friend of mine in Benares and said, "Mr. Jackson, you're a friend of mine. I want to ask you a confidential question. What and where is America?" We are inclined to laugh at the naïve question of the pundit, but our incipient laughter gives way to very sober and solemn reflection, "Yes, just what is America? And where is it? Where is it going? And where is it now?"

What and Where Is America?

Someone in India, a little under the influence of liquor, said to me: "So you're an American? How funny!" Yes, it is "funny" that I am an American, that any of us is an American. I held up a piece of a black pepper vine before an audience of 45,000 in Travancore, India, and said: "This pepper vine is the reason for my being an American. Columbus sailed after this pepper and discovered America." In a way that was true. The economic interpretation of history has a truth in it. But is that all? Does a search for spices account for *this?* In and through all the driving motives of a lower kind was there the guiding hand of Providence, separating a people from the Old World to begin a new experiment, that through this fresh beginning the Old World itself might in turn be made new? Is it true, as someone has suggested—though we dare not repeat it, except upon our knees—that "America is humanity's last chance?" Its last chance for reconstruction? I am not sure about the "last chance," but I am sure that it is the latest. For here a divine purpose seems to be working out, a purpose that may come to fruition at this fluid period of the world's history.

What is America? Tall skyscrapers blotting out the horizon and the stars, bulging pockets, the go-getter type, a boasting upstart pushing for world supremacy? All of us who love America have seen all that in it and have felt ashamed, but we have seen something more—as Paul said of the slave Onesimus, "no longer a mere slave but something more." (Philemon 16—Moffatt.) We see the "something more": the slavery to material things is there, but there is something breaking the chains, something making for freedom for itself and others, something down underneath that won't be suppressed. What is that something that constitutes the real America?

That something did not begin in the beginnings of America, but was introduced later. The first colony planted in America, the Virginia Colony, was too mixed up with the old to be the agent of this something new. According to the historians Charles and Mary Beard, "The great [London] Company that planted the first successful colony represented . . . the dominant elements in English commercial life. Its stock was advertised in the pulpit as well as in the market places, and subscriptions were made in the interests of religion, patriotism, and profit." Religion was there, but it was aristocratic religion, baptizing and sponsoring commercialism and imperialism. It is true that Captain John Smith declared, in reference to the Indians, that the first duty of Virginians was "to preach, baptise into the Christian religion, and by the propagation of the Gospel to recover out of the arms of the devil, a number of poor and miserable souls wrapt up unto death in almost invincible ignorance." But they were also to enslave them! They were to Christianize and enslave the Indians. But the freedom-loving Indians wouldn't allow them to do that.

Moreover this type of Christianity with which Virginia began showed the same attitudes toward classes as it did toward races. In the churches congregations were seated according to age and social position and estate. One Virginia family made the commoners "wait outside the church until the superiors were duly seated in the large pew especially provided for them." Among the 105 first settlers about one half were "gentlemen," and only four were carpenters. Religion baptized and backed aristocracy. Out of that soil the American dream could not and did not arise. It belonged to the decaying old. It is true that out of that unlikely soil arose one who sponsored the American dream and gave it shape—Jefferson. But he was a root out of dry ground. Moreover he sponsored and gave shape to something that was born elsewhere.

Where was the American dream born? It was conceived in the Mayflower Compact, was born in Rhode Island, grew up in Pennsylvania, became of age and legalized in Jefferson, and came to embodiment in Lincoln.

It was conceived in the Mayflower Compact. When the Pilgrims found themselves landing on the shores of New England, they thought they would be under the authority of the Charter of Virginia. When they found that the Charter of Virginia did not extend that far, it dawned on them that they were under no authority. The reaction to this realization, especially on the part of those taken on in England, was: "We are under no authority? We'll have none! We'll be free from all authority." A false and abortive and undisciplined democracy was about to be conceived. But the answer of the Pilgrims was swift and headed that off: "If we have no authority from without, then we will take it on ourselves from within." In the words of the Compact they would make "just & equall lawes, . . . unto which we promise all due submission and obedience." "Just & equall lawes!" Laws in the Old World had not been "just" for they had not been "equall"; there was one law for "gentlemen" and another for commoners. But here in the Mayflower Compact democracy was conceived. However, it could not come to birth in the Massachusetts Colony. That colony belonged to the old. Governor Winthrop of the

Massachusetts Colony said, "The meanest and most contemptible form of government is that of democracy." There is a statute upon the books of Massachusetts, placed there in colonial days, "forbidding the common people to wear the clothes of gentry as not befitting their station in life." Democracy could not come to birth in that atmosphere. Religion was Puritan, but it was purified only in spots; through its narrowness and intolerances it too belonged to the old.

Only in Rhode Island could democracy come to birth. The smallest state of the union gave us the largest concept. The credit must go to the Baptists and to the Quakers. They thought thoughts of God as Father, therefore of men as brothers, therefore equal in the sight of God; if equal in the sight of God, then equal in the sight of man; if equal in the sight of man, then democracy as the political expression of that equalitarianism before God and man. Democracy was founded on a world view—a view of God, consequently of man, consequently of government. "Democracy is the political expression of Christianity," says Thomas Mann. Democracy was born out of the Christian faith. Will it survive the decay of that faith? If the root withers, will the fruit continue? I doubt it. If God becomes marginal, noncreative in our collective life, we will go the way Europe has gone. When God faded out of Europe—remember one Russian writer said, "Europe has lost Christ, and Europe will perish"—men could not stand the emptiness, the sheer meaninglessness and goallessness of life. They had to have something to obey, something to command them, something to which they could be supremely loyal. Since they had lost God, they turned to the half-gods—the half-gods of state as in Fascism, of race as in Nazism, and of class—the class of the proletariat—as in Communism. When God departed, the half-gods took over. If God departs from us, then we will turn to some half-god, probably some form of fascism in the guise of an antifascism, and will say, "Command us." "He who will not be governed by God will be governed by tyrants," said William Penn. Democracy is the offspring of the Christian faith and is being nurtured at its breasts; it will not survive the death of its mother.

But democracy born in Rhode Island could not grow up there. The situation was too mixed. The best atmosphere in which it could grow up was in Pennsylvania amid the purer faith of the Quakers. The Quakers were the leaven of the situation. They were the first to forbid their members to keep slaves; they gave "the first circulating library, the first medical school and hospital, the first fire company, the earliest municipal improvement, and the first legal journal." Penn's principles of government were the highest which had been enunciated up to that time. Woolman declared the principle that "the Creator of the earth is the owner of it." His plea for the poor was not published for thirty years. Charles and Mary Beard say of him: "In the writings of this simple workman, born on American soil in the reign of George II, are to be found the roots of American intellectual radicalism."

But while Quakerism could provide the cultural ground for the growth of democracy, only in Jefferson did it really come to voice. Here comes into view a part of the contradiction of American life. Democracy was born out of the Christian faith and nurtured by its principles wherever they were rediscovered, and yet it was voiced by a Jefferson who got his ideas of democracy partly from the Christian faith and partly from the French secularists. In the voicing of that democracy, while the Christian faith was acknowledged, the heavy end of the emphasis was on the secular side. Herein is one of the crisis moments of American life. Christianity began to be tolerated as a marginal factor; secularism began to take control. The Declaration of Independence mentions God; the Constitution does not. In dealing with Tripoli, President Washington allowed it to be squarely stated that "the government of the United States is not in any sense founded on the Christian religion." And yet the Christian faith gave birth to this democracy. Here lies the area of the great confusion and the great contradiction. Two forces, democracy and Christianity, belonging together, are in the process of being separated. That separation has continued. It is with us still. Christianity will be tolerated on the margin, but will not be allowed to be creative and dynamic at the center. A recent cartoon sums up the situation: Uncle Sam, standing on the Ship of State, says to the representatives of the Christian faith, "It is your business to keep off from the Ship of State the barnacles of greed, selfishness, and dishonesty." And that was supposed to be a compliment to religion! It was to keep off the barnacles, but it was to have nothing to say about the directing of the ship; it was to make it smooth-running, but secular forces would provide the chart and decide the destination and run the ship. Religion was to be an appendage brought in to get rid of appendages.

What took place in the government took place in nearly every phase of American life. Secularism took over education, business, race relations, and international policies. Religion might influence and soften, but it could not guide and direct. That isn't quite fair, for individuals and groups here and there leaven these various phases of our collective life with Christian influence and character, and in many ways have been the saving salt of the situation. But in the main the life of America in its collective phases was secularized; secular motives dominated, and a secular spirit prevailed.

But if we have taken grudgingly to Christianity we have also taken grudgingly to democracy. We have tried to compartmentalize it in the political and keep it out of the economic and the social and the international. Both Christianity and democracy have fought for every inch of ground they have gained in the soul of America. For America is not truly Christian, nor is it truly democratic. It is a nation fighting with itself, for it itself is a contradiction.

The contradiction runs through all of American life. Someone has facetiously said that the Pilgrims in landing on the shores of America fell on their knees and then on the aborigines. That remark is not facetious; it is a fact. The Pilgrims came for liberty of conscience, and yet the capitalists who financed their pilgrimage expected to get back large financial returns. "To protect masters against violence [by slaves] a drastic code was adopted prescribing whipping, branding, ear-clipping, castration, and death for various offenses; but the consolations of the Christian faith were not withheld, for the law, while denying the right of manumission, expressly authorized baptism." After the "War for Sailors' Rights" fought with Britain in 1812, the shipowners reduced wages of sailors until in a few decades they brought them below those possible for American workmen. The Boston Marine Society, composed of the most respected shipowners of Boston, at a time when the North was being inflamed over the cruelty to the Negro in the South, petitioned the government to restore the right to flog sailors to their work. In New England factory hours for young and old were from twelve to fourteen hours a day. The owners contended that "the morals of the operatives will necessarily suffer if longer absent from the wholesome discipline of factory life." The contradiction and the consequent conflict were in us.

Perhaps the most fundamental struggle in our national life is the struggle between the rights of property and the rights of persons. Hamilton stood for the rights of property, and Jefferson stood for the rights of the people. They were symbols of an internal struggle. Webster was the spokesman for property. "He believed that the form and frame of governments were determined by the nature and distribution of property, that American institutions were founded on property, and that property ought to have a direct representation in the government." Arguing against manhood suffrage he said that "all the revolutions of history which had shaken society to its foundations had been revolts against property; that equal suffrage was incompatible with inequality in property and if adopted would either end in assaults on wealth or new restraints on democracy—a reaction of the notables." Religion, as embodied in some of its spokesmen, threw itself on the side of property and became hysterical over the rise of the people. Dr. Timothy Dwight, president of Yale, could say: "If Jefferson is elected we may see our wives and daughters the victims of legal prostitution, soberly dishonored, speciously polluted; the outcasts of delicacy and virtue, the loathing of God and man." This struggle between property and the people has continued to this day. James Truslow Adams says: "As America grew she tried to serve, so to say, God and Mammon—that is, she insisted upon clinging to the ideal of Jeffersonianism while gathering in the money profits from Hamiltonianism."

That battle is still far from being resolved. Property privilege speaks through the lips of Frederick Townsend Martin as he testifies before a government investigating committee: "We are not politicians or public thinkers; we are the rich; we own America; we got it, God knows how, but we intend to keep it if we can by throwing all the tremendous weight of our support, our influence, our money, our political connections, our purchased senators, our hungry congressmen, our public-speaking demagogues into the scale against any legislature, any political platform, any presidential campaign that threatens the integrity of our estate." This statement is serious in view of the fact that about fifteen per cent of the people own about eighty-five per cent of the wealth of this land. And they are far more willing to sacrifice people than they are to sacrifice property in this world crisis. Conscription of the persons of our young people was not seriously opposed, but conscription of property would have been bitterly opposed had the government dared to propose it. A ceiling was put on prices and on wages; but when a ceiling was proposed of $25,000 yearly income, after all taxes were paid, the spokesmen for property carried the day, and the proposal was thrown out. Property sat tight. The action of Congress in refusing this limit of income in a national crisis was, in fact, a sowing of the seeds of revolution against privilege and property. It was an expensive thing to do and will cost property and privilege more than it gave to them. For the millions whose persons have been conscripted are going to ask an accounting when they return.

Do not misunderstand me. I am not against property and privilege. I want more of both—for everybody. I want wealth, not concentrated in the hands of the few, but widely distributed to the many. Wealth and privilege are like manure: concentrate it in one pile and it is an evil-smelling mass, but distribute it across the fields and it results in abundant harvests. Wealth and privilege concentrated in the hands of the few is a festering mass, but distributed to the many it results in a stable and truly prosperous civilization.

What and where is America? America is a dream—unfulfilled. A dream of equality of opportunity, of privilege and property widely distributed; a dream of a place where class is abolished and where a man is a man, a place where race and birth and color are transcended by the fact of a common brotherhood, a place where humanity as humanity can begin again a fresh experiment in human brotherhood that will be a new beginning for the race as a whole, a place where all our gifts and resources are held not for ourselves alone but as instruments of service for the rest of humanity —that is the dream. Part of it has been fulfilled, perhaps better fulfilled than in any other place on our planet. But that isn't saying much. For the most of our planet is an unsatisfactory mess. Our good is good, but it isn't good enough. For our gold is full of alloy. Our democracy is full of special privilege. Democracy has been the moral shield behind which selfish interests have worked. We are shot through and through with unreality.

A newspaper advertisement offers "skunk-dyed opossum furs"; that is the symbol of much of American life—camouflaged unreality. Wooden ducks are upon our lawns; wooden porters stand to welcome you at the porch; we have wooden woodpeckers for door knockers; glass coal with electric bulbs beneath in the fireplaces; up-to-date houses made to look old and antique; complexions plastered; stockings painted on; hair with kinks provided if you haven't any, kinks taken out if God has given them to you; adventures in the movie by proxy, life at second hand clicking before you; the use of drugs and narcotics growing by leaps and bounds to keep up the supposed happiness and the supposed morale; the freedom of woman turned into a freedom to guzzle stupefying drinks at bars and to puff poisonous fumes everywhere; radios giving out canned music and canned speeches to a people growing more and more mechanical as they are shaped by mechanics—a people being made from the image of God into the image of things. Is that America? Was the Hindu right when he wrote a reply to *Mother India* and entitled it *Uncle Sham?*

Yes, and no! We must bow our heads and acknowledge with shame the unreality. And yet, and yet something within us says that this unreality is the camouflage, that down underneath the soul of this people is essentially sound, that democracy still lives as the one valid dream—unfulfilled, yes, but the thing that *has* us.

This soundness I have seen in youth. "I would trust the moral reactions of my students," said the principal of a large high school, "far more than I would the moral reactions of the forty-year-olds. They never strike a false moral note." I have asked across this country from high-school principals if they ever have known the young people to elect a rotter, a bad character, as the president of the student body. The answer invariably has been, "Never." This shows a moral soundness. And greater still, I have seen the young people elect a Japanese-American or a Negro as president of their student body. That shows an essential democratic soundness.

But this soundness is also seen in the more mature. A friend of mine does the buying for a great corporation and spends a million dollars a day, and yet himself lives in simplicity, and has a strong sense of stewardship. A close friend of a presidential candidate, he said to him after the election: "Do you know why you were not elected president? The reason, as I see it, is this: The presidents of the United States are elected by the crossroads Methodists and Baptists —the common garden variety of religious people. You did not get them. In your opening address you talked as though you were talking to a cattle market. You sounded no great moral note. You lost them, and so you lost the election." My friend may have been wrong in fastening on that as the particular reason in this particular case, but he was right in insisting that the soul of America is deeply religious and that to sound the moral note gets an essential and widespread response. And this not merely among the crossroads, semieducated portions of our country. At this point in my writing I was called to answer a long-distance telephone call asking me to give the opening address in a state teachers convention, the theme of the convention being, "Faith of our fathers, living still." That faith was living still at the heart of secular education in the state of Missouri, and the teachers announced it as their convention theme. The Christian faith is woven into the texture of our national culture and cannot be eradicated.

The spokesmen of big business feel the same pull of that conviction. Roger Babson, the business expert, was asked by the President of Brazil what the essential difference is between North and South America. Why has the United States with no greater resources than Brazil gone so far ahead and Brazil, and in fact all Latin American countries, lagged far behind? To which Mr. Babson replied: "The reason is probably this: North America was largely founded by people seeking God. South America was founded by men seeking gold." To which the President of Brazil replied, "I believe you are right." Religion is prevalent in Latin America, but it has been magical religion; in North America religion, on the whole, has been moral religion. It has been a morally cleansing power. And that is important, for the whole of the outer structure of life rests on character. If the character breaks, the confidence breaks; if the confidence breaks, the country breaks. Speaking to President Roosevelt on behalf of a group I said: "You are trying to change the outer structure of this country, and some of us are trying to change the inner structure. And we think that the whole of the outer structure rests on the inner, on that imponderable thing called character. We therefore think that our task is not unimportant; in fact we humbly think it is all-important."

The oldest living city in the world is said to be Damascus. The reason it has survived the decay of many cities is that there is a stream of cleansing going through and under it all the time. A river, arising on Mount Hermon, flows down through it, running along its gutters, bubbling up in its fountains, and perpetually cleansing the city generally. If our democracy has survived, and has survived with increasing power, it is because underneath the life of our country has been flowing the cleansing stream of the Christian faith. It has been grudgingly obeyed, but to the degree that it has been obeyed it has been cleansing and character-making. To the degree that that faith is operative in our national life, to that degree will our nation be sound, and consequently lasting. When that faith decays, our country, founded on it, will decay with it.

What, then, is America? It is a possibility—and a portent. It is a possibility. For here nearly all the nations of the earth have gathered and have become one nation. The blood of all the world is in our veins. If we succeed, then all the world succeeds with us, for we are the world—in miniature. If we succeed, the rest of the world need not be jealous, for we are they. And we can succeed only as our success becomes a benefit to them. If it does not, we have not succeeded— we have failed ourselves and them. America is God's experimental ground, his demonstration center, where he has brought representatives of all the world to try out, on a small scale, corporate living. If these representatives of all the world can live together in a sound, enlightened, and progressive way, as one family, then the rest of the world can lift up its head in hope; for the experiment, having been demonstrated and proved possible, can be applied to the world. If it proves possible in the microcosm, it may prove possible in the macrocosm. The world can live together, for it does live together—in us. We are the world's proving ground. As we go, the world goes.

We are, then, a possibility—and a portent. For we may fail God, man, and ourselves. And whether we will or not has not yet been settled. We let the world down once. We may do it again. Our spokesman Woodrow Wilson voiced the voice of real America as he spoke for us at the end of the last war. We thrilled to it, and the world thrilled to it. Hope and faith were in the air; we were on the verge of new beginnings. And then the atmosphere changed. We played petty party politics. This unreal, this false America with which we are fighting leaped into the saddle and rode us back to our fears and to our selfishnesses and pretended isolations. We let the world drift into its second catastrophe. Now we have come to a new crisis—the crisis of reconstruction. Is this America Christian enough and democratic enough to reshape herself and the future of the world? The fate of humanity probably depends on the answer to that question. Walt Whitman sums it all up in these words to America:

How can I pierce the impenetrable blank of the future?
I feel thy ominous greatness evil as well as good.

Chapter IV—

THE SEVEN HESITATIONS OF DEMOCRACY

WHEN THE DECLARATION OF INDEPENDENCE was written these words were used: "All men are created equal, . . . endowed by their Creator with certain unalienable Rights." When that word "all" was written into that sentence, little did the authors know how it would live to disturb and awaken the soul of this people. The word "all" was inevitable, for there would not have been democracy if it had been left out; but, once in, it has become the most explosive and revolutionary word in our national history.

We have had trouble with that word "all." We cannot let it go, and we cannot let go to it. It will not let us rest until we say the words "all men" with complete abandon and with no reservations. The history of our struggling with that word "all" is the history of the progress of America, and our future progress depends upon what we do with it.

One of the basic reasons for our not giving equality to "all" is our fundamental doubt of the proposition itself that "all men are created equal." We do not really believe they are "equal." And they are not! Not intrinsically, for there are real differences in endowment. Herbert Agar suggests that "all men are equal in God," which is good if a man has a vivid sense of God—but if he doesn't? And most men don't! Then the equality in God drops away, and bare inequalities stand out in stark reality. It seems to me that democracy should be founded, not on the proposition that all men are equal, but that all men should have equality of opportunity. I remember how in a hotel room in Seattle some years ago this phrase, familiar to me before, came with a sense of significance, of warm and decisive meaning; it seemed the basic phrase, for it contained the basic idea. Equality of opportunity is the birthright of every man, and society can give that. Whether the man, given equality of opportunity, gains the other equalities of character and achievement and standing is up to him. Equality of opportunity is a birthright; the other equalities are achievements. Democracy must give equal access to education, to culture, to meaningful employment, to political rights and power, to leisure, to adequate housing, to know and to achieve the highest. Society gives the access; the man gives the achievement.

Having acknowledged differences in individuals, that they are not equal in endowment, I hasten to add that there are no fundamental differences between classes or races. Down underneath surface differences of class and race there is a fundamental humanity. There are no permanently inferior classes or races; there are only undeveloped classes and races. All classes and, all races are capable of the same general development if given the same stimulus and the same opportunity. The differences between classes and races are not biological but cultural. If that is true, then this gives us hope for humanity. Every class and race is capable of infinite development. But we have hesitated to commit ourselves to giving equality of opportunity to everybody. The diehards within us die hard—and expensively.

American democracy has had seven great hesitations in regard to that word "all":

1. *The hesitation as to whether we should take in the territories beyond the original colonies on the basis of equality or make them subordinate.* The pattern prevalent at the time, and still prevalent, was to have a seat of empire, with outlying places subordinate to and exploited for the benefit of that seat of empire. In America we could have done the same thing, and the temptation to do so was very strong and compelling. To take in these territories on the same basis as the original nucleus was fought at every step, and this in high places.

Dr. Timothy Dwight, president of Yale University (1795-1817), said of the people of the Ohio Valley: "They are not fit to live in regular society. They are too idle; too talkative; too passionate; too prodigal; and too shiftless to acquire either property or character. They are impatient at the restraints of law, religion, or morality; grumble about the taxes," and so on. To take in the people of Ohio on the basis of equality and apply the word "all" to them seemed the beginning of the end. And yet Ohio has given more presidents to the United States than any other state; in fact, more than all New England, from which Timothy Dwight spoke so loftily.

And when Louisiana was about to be taken in as an equal, Josiah Quincy voiced these words of hesitation and protest to Congress: "You have no authority to throw the rights and property of this people into the hotch-potch with the wild men on the Missouri, nor with the mixed, though more respectable race of Anglo-Hispan-Gallo-Americans who bask on the sands at the mouth of the Mississippi.

... Do you suppose the people of the Northern and Atlantic States will, or ought to, look on with patience and see Representatives and Senators from the Red River and Missouri, pouring themselves upon this and the other floor, managing the concerns of a seaboard fifteen hundred miles, at least, from their residence?" And yet "the wild men on the Missouri" are today as cultured and contributive as any we have in the union!

But this word "all" pressed upon this intellectual and cultural snobbery and won decisive ground when it was decided that territories should become states on the basis of full equality. That step was one of the greatest in human history. Had we tried to build up an imperialism centering in the original colonies we should have had a situation in America similar to what we have in a large part of the world: one portion sitting on a lid, suppressing the other portion, and solemnly telling why they cannot get off the lid—the trusteeship must be maintained, and besides if they did get off the lid there would be civil war among those under the lid. So we must sit tight—as tight as one may sit who sits on a volcano!

That simple but profound solution to the problem, namely the giving of complete equality to territories, may prove the norm for a world pattern. The world will fight it—as we did—but in the end we shall have to come to it, for it is right. And whatever is right is stable, and whatever is wrong is unstable. The world is in a state of instability because of the refusal of this simple principle. We took it, made the adventure in spite of many a hesitation, and gained a union. We took counsel of our faith instead of our fear, and time has amply justified that adventure of faith in people. Every time we took in a new territory we were enriched. The center of democracy is not on the Atlantic Seaboard where the original colonies were, but it is in the great Middle West.

2. *The second hesitation about applying the word "all" was in regard to one half the population within the union —namely, to women.* That hesitation to give full equality to women has been long and agonizing. We gave the right to vote to the "degenerates" of the Ohio Valley and to "the wild men on the Missouri" long before we gave it to women. Speaking on this subject recently, I found on the front seat a lady who had been in jail for two weeks because she had picketed the White House asking for votes for women. And she was not an elderly woman either!

And yet women, if the property qualification were the criterion, as Webster suggested, would have seventy-five per cent of the votes of America, for they own seventy-five per cent of the wealth! And they do ninety per cent of the purchasing! All of which seems to be a divine joke played on the men for their snobberies and assumed superiorities. The meek are inheriting the earth!

We have hesitated to apply the word "all" to women, and yet it was a woman who started all this stream of Christian and democratic civilization in the West. The "man of Macedonia" was a woman! When Paul answered the cry of the "man of Macedonia" to come over to Europe to "help us," the first convert was a woman, "Lydia, a seller of purple"—a businesswoman. She certainly started something! And yet man has coolly assumed possession of that movement, as if he were the author and the finisher of the whole process. The fact is that he was not the author, and apparently he is not to be the finisher; for according to Benjamin Kidd, the sociologist, women are to be "the psychic center of power in the future." Note, not the physical, nor the intellectual center of power, but the "psychic center." Why? Women, says Kidd, embody the co-operative spirit. It is their function to create a co-operative order out of diverse elements in a home. Man stands for competition; he goes out and competes with nature and his fellow man to gain a living. The future belongs to co-operation; the competitive principle has run its course.

If the future belongs to co-operation and women represent the co-operative spirit, then women are to be, in literal fact, the psychic center of power in that future. And with seventy-five per cent of the wealth and ninety per cent of the purchasing power in their hands, the prediction has very material backing! Where do men come in? They come in as they are converted—converted from selfish competition to co-operation. Fortunately they are convertible! All of which may sound like playful banter. But in reality it is the solemn truth. Man will have to give complete equality to woman or find the nemesis of history working out as it now seems to be working out. The handwriting on the wall is plain: deny the word "all" to anyone and it slips through your own fingers—you've lost it to the one to whom you deny it. Russia has gone far beyond us in the place it habitually gives to women and is, in this respect, therefore further advanced than Western democracies.

3. *The third great hesitation in the application of "all" is in regard to the most important group in our democracy —namely, the children.* Man has been physically the stronger, came first to power, and has conceded with reluctance any

part of that power to the physically weaker portions of society, the women and the children. Children have only slowly come to their own. Jesus set the child "in the midst"; we set him on the edges, or worse. The Roman father had the right of life and death over his child. The infant was presented to the father at birth, and he looked it over to see whether or not he wanted to keep it—worked its arms and its legs to see whether they worked well. If he didn't like the child, he broke its back over his knee and threw it out. We have come a long way since then, but not the full way. Child labor laws have been fought by exploiting greed. The child is called on to assume his share in the reshaping of the national life only in an emergency like war. He is called on to fight three years sooner than he is allowed to vote. This war has now become "a kids' war." But only in the execution of it. The older generation do all the blunderings into war and do all the top-position management of it, and "the kids" bear the brunt—the bloody end of things. And then after the war the older generation will shape the peace conditions under which the younger generation must live. Since they must bear the heavy end of things in a crisis, they must be allowed to help shape things for the ordinary days ahead.

When I paid a surprise visit to a school in Russia and asked for the privilege of talking to a class, I was sent to a class made up of twelve- or thirteen-year-olds. I asked them what they had in favor of this regime. A sea of hands went up, and they eagerly told why they favored it. Their answers were intelligent and to the point. Then I asked them what they had against the regime. A few hands went up. "We still have a good many of the bourgeois left in our system; we must clear them out." "The government gives good orders, but the bourgeois still left change them and thus often throw confusion into our regime." I reminded them that they were not criticizing the system; they were only criticizing within the system. What had they against the system itself? A look of incredulity went over their faces that I should ask such a question. A little hand went up, and a piping voice excitedly said, "But sir, we have nothing against the system. The system is all right." The child pronounced the system all right. That conviction laid in the child mind has proved to be one of the most important facts in human history; it held Russia steady in her hour of awful crisis and defeat. Convictions laid in the mind of the child last—the only really lasting ones. Christian democracy will not last unless the child inwardly accepts it because it is reasonable and right, and, more important still, because he is a functioning part of it. He will not understand it unless he understands it from within, and he will not understand it from within by verbal instruction alone. He must be vitally a part of it; it must function where he is concerned. He must learn it by experience both as object and agent.

This we have not done—not really, except here and there. We have applied the word "all" to children grudgingly and with hesitation.

4. *The fourth hesitation about the application of the word "all" is in regard to another group in our midst—labor.* We have seen the struggle between the rights of property and the rights of people in our democracy. Madison tried to put them together in declaring that "the first object of government" is the protection of "the diversity in the facul-

ties of men, from which the rights of property originate."
That statement itself represents the struggle in the soul of a
man, and in the soul of a nation. The first object of government is to protect the diversity in the faculties of men—
not the men themselves, but the diversity in their faculties—
in order to protect the diversity in the rights of property—in
other words, the right to unequal property. Property and
not the person was the end. The statement is heavily loaded
on the side of property, and of unequal property at that.
That has been the emphasis in our national life—property
before persons, capital before labor. This was vividly illus-
trated by the Legislature of California, which made it a
felony to steal a tire but only a misdemeanor to desert a
wife—property more important than the person.

Capital owns the tools of production; it therefore has
the right to hire and fire labor. Property, not the person,
has the last word. The right to collective bargaining has
been grudgingly conceded, or conceded not at all, in American industry, though Britain has adopted it for some time
on an almost universal scale. The refusal of the right of
collective bargaining brings an inequality which can be
seen in an individual workman standing at the factory
gate with dinner pail in hand. He stands there to bargain
with this giant corporation. He has, perhaps, two days' re-
serve food behind him; the corporation has reserves of
millions. How could they bargain on terms of equality?
The corporation can bargain collectively—it does so, as a
corporation—and yet the right of labor to bargain collectively is only grudgingly conceded, or not at all.

Socially the man who labors and the man who owns the
capital are not equal. The one is low-caste and the other

high-caste. "I am so grateful that you have received me on the same social level as the rest, although I am a working-woman," said a fine-appearing woman as she was about to leave our Ashram. I was inwardly shocked that she should feel that way. But it was revealing that she did feel that way. There was a reason, and the reason was that we have very grudgingly extended equality to those who labor.

5. *The fifth great hesitation has been to extend equality to those of another color.* We have discriminated against those whose skins happen to be pigmented, no matter what their characters and abilities may be. This matter of color is a strange thing. We love varieties of color in nature and balk at it in human nature. We balk at it from both sides. The name for "white" in an African language means "decayed," "on the verge of rotting." Some white and colored children were playing together in harmony and enjoyment when the white father, a minister, called down to one of the larger colored children to be careful not to break his boy's velocipede. Later the little fellow came to his father and said, "Daddy, they didn't like what you said to them. They called you names. They said you were 'an old whitey.'" It works both ways! Someday we shall give up our prejudices from both sides, and we shall see just a person, for that is the meaning of democracy. To make democracy mean the rule of the white is to abandon democracy and to adopt snobocracy. If you do not extend democracy to everybody, you cannot hold it for anybody. Its very nature has changed.

I was in a city in the North when some school children were taking the pledge of allegiance to the flag, a ceremony that always gets me to the depths. Seldom have greater words been put together than the words, "One Nation, indivisible, with liberty and justice for all." That is the very essence of democracy. But I gasped as these children repeated these noble words. I said to myself, "How can they say that, 'With liberty and justice for all'? They haven't liberty; they are bound by all sorts of restrictions and segregations other people are not bound by, and they certainly do not get justice in our democracy—for they are colored." A teacher told me how they were able to say it: they added under their breath two words, "With liberty and justice for all *but me*." A nation that makes a part of its citizenry repeat its pledge of allegiance with that addition is denying the central postulate on which that democracy is founded. We must change that situation, or we must change our pledge of allegiance and make it read, "With liberty and justice for some"—in which case democracy is renounced.

I was in a city in the South. It was primary election day, but since there was only one party it was the real election day. The Negroes were disfranchised by the simple expedient of asking, when they came to register, whether they had voted the Democratic ticket in 1876. No whites were asked that question. The Negroes protested, but got no satisfaction. That night in a public mass meeting for whites I announced before my address that I had an "obituary notice" to read which would come as a shock to the friends of the deceased: "Democracy died today in the city of ——— when American citizens were denied the right of suffrage because of the color of their skins. To those who have eyes to see, the ballot box will henceforth be draped in mourning." I expected a wave of anger and bowed my head for the storm. I was prepared to take it. Instead, the reaction was sorrow —sorrow that we could do that in our democracy. You could almost squeeze tears out of the atmosphere. To the credit of the newspapers, they wrote it up with front-page headlines: "Reads Obituary for Democracy in ———," and they wrote it up favorably. And further, twenty-five leading citizens signed a petition urging the Democratic State Convention to change this unjust discrimination.

The head of a Negro college said to me that he was anxious about his people—they were inwardly disgruntled, growingly so. And then he gave this instance: He was in a movie, and everyone arose to sing "America" as it was flashed on the screen. Everybody sang except the Negroes; they did not sing. Why? They were not able to sing, "Sweet land of liberty," for it was not to them a land of liberty, but a land of segregations, of constant reminders of their "place" —subordination. So they did not sing. A very intelligent and cultured Negro said as he left our Ashram group, where we had lived together for two weeks on the basis of complete equality and brotherhood: "For the first time in my life I've lived inwardly relaxed and without fear. Now as I leave this group and go into the outside world I must watch my step lest I run against those invisible walls surrounding me everywhere." Those invisible walls! Democracy cannot have invisible walls for some and open freedom for others—not if it is to remain democracy. It cannot have a part of its citizenry able to sing,

> My country 'tis of thee
> Sweet land of liberty,

and another part unable to sing it because liberty is denied.

There are two Americas. One is the America of freedom,

the lover of liberty, the believer in democracy. That America I love. Under God, it has my complete loyalty. But there is another America—and it is not sectional; it is found in both North and South—which would deny that freedom and democracy and would have us say, "With liberty and justice for all white people." That America I do not love. It does not have my loyalty. For this is a false America, a traitorous America, and a greater danger to our democracy than Hitlerism. For it is Hitlerism right in our own midst. Hitler believes in racial arrogances; so does this false America—they are blood brothers. I repudiate both. I want America to be the real America—the America of "liberty and justice for all." America is now a split personality—at war with herself.

If the objection is made that we cannot give equality, that it must be achieved, then the reply is that we can give equality of opportunity; the achievement of the rest of the equalities is up to the Negro. I was addressing a huge Negro mass meeting and quoted the statement of Mr. Charlie Spaulding, the founder and head of a great Negro life insurance company: "Equality is not a thing that should be demanded, because it cannot be granted. It has to be earned. . . . If the Negro wants equality, except equality of opportunity, he must pay for it, and the unalterable price is character and achievement." A dead silence fell over that great audience. "Equality is not a thing that should be demanded, because it cannot be granted"—those words fell like a pall upon their souls. I hastened to add: "Mr. Spaulding says, 'If the Negro wants equality, except equality of opportunity . . .' That, as I understand it, is the only equality the Negro is demanding—equality of opportunity. Give him that and he will take care of the rest of the

78

equalities by his own character and achievement." That audience burst into an approving applause—an applause that registered a position. That and that alone is what the Negro is demanding, and that and that alone we can—and ought to—give. To hesitate to give it means that we hesitate to believe in and act according to our own democracy. In that case to talk about democracy is hypocrisy.

America's power and influence in the world will be determined by her ability to set her own house in order, and thus to act up to her democracy.

6. *The sixth great hesitation in applying the word "all" is in regard to those of Asiatic origin in our midst.* There have been two basic discriminations in regard to these people. The first was in the matter of immigration. Had we put them on the same quota basis as the rest of the world (two per cent of the 1890 census) there would have been only about 350 people coming into America each year from all Asia—India, China, Japan. This small quota would never be an economic problem in a nation of 130,000,000. In that case we could stop the smuggling across the borders of Canada and Mexico. The nations concerned would be in a psychological position to help us to stop illegal entry. Now we cannot ask them to do so, for we have humiliated them by this discrimination. We have a right to limit immigration, but we have no right to humiliate others. Such attitudes and practices deny our own democracy and sow the seeds of war. This discrimination was one of the causes that led to the war with Japan. A few years ago I said to President Roosevelt in regard to putting the Asiatic nations on the same quota basis as the rest of the world: "I know nothing that you can do that will help right our relations with

the East, and particularly with Japan, more than just this simple act." But we procrastinated and hesitated, and—!

The second basic discrimination was in regard to the Japanese-Americans after war began. This group of Americans had one of the best records of any group in our land. They had proportionately more young people in college than any other racial group in American life; they had a larger percentage to volunteer for the American armed forces than any other—at this time of writing there are over ten thousand in the Army, forty-eight of whom have received the decoration of the Order of the Purple Heart; their crime percentage was the lowest; there were almost none on relief during the depression; there has been no known case of sabotage by the Japanese on the West Coast according to the F.B.I., and Secretary Stimson says there has been no known case of sabotage by the Japanese in Hawaii. Yet with that record we put citizens and noncitizens behind barbed wires. At the same time we allowed a million German and Italian aliens to be free on that same coast. One Japanese businessman was in partnership with an Italian. He was put into a camp, and the Italian stayed and ran the business. If we say we did it for their protection, then the answer is that it would have paid us to plant a soldier at every Japanese house for protective purposes until the loyal and the disloyal could be weeded out. We put them behind barbed wires with almost nothing to do, fed them at the taxpayers' expense—the total expense ran to $80,000,000 a year. All over the country farms were being abandoned by the thousands—78,000 farms have been abandoned—with no one to run them, and here we put some of the best farmers of the world behind barbed wire to sit in comparative idleness. As I walked over one of these camps I said to the superintendent: "This is a monument to American stupidity." "I entirely agree with you," was his reply. "Help save our wavering faith in democracy," said one of the Japanese pastors to me. My blood ran cold as I heard Japanese-American high-school young people in these camps take the pledge of allegiance to the flag, "With liberty and justice for all." A Caucasian teacher turned to me and said, "There's your 'all' again."

The real America is coming to the surface and is trying to undo the wrong done to these loyal Americans and is trying to relocate them across the country. But the damage to democracy has been done. The only ones who will come out of this with undamaged souls are the Christians. For real Christians have learned the secret of living *in spite of* when they cannot live *on account of*. I never have had more responsive audiences than when speaking to audiences as large as seven thousand in these camps on the subject "The Christian Answer to Suffering, Merited and Unmerited." They didn't want sympathy; they wanted a philosophy of life that could take hold of justice and injustice and take them up into the purpose of their lives and not merely bear them but use them—make them contribute. "You have raised the morale of this camp one hundred per cent by that message," wrote a Japanese. People who can respond to that kind of appeal have something in them. If the Christians come out of this unsoured they will show us a new type of Christianity. As it is, they are captivating their captors. The superintendent and two other Caucasian American officials were converted by the Christian life of one of these Japanese-Americans in the camp. I asked an

American soldier guarding the entrance gate to one of these camps, "Have any trouble?" His face lighted up, "Not a bit. They are wonderful people to work with." They are. And they will make excellent citizens. We must cease discrimination against those of Asiatic origin in our midst, and that of course includes, and especially includes, the Chinese and the East Indians.

Three times I have been refused as I offered payment for service done. Once when I offered a Japanese redcap payment for carrying my luggage to a cab he said, "No thank you; welcome to Portland." He was a Christian and had a daughter in the Amsterdam Youth Conference. Another time I tried to pay a Chinese restaurant keeper: "No thank you; you are a friend of China's." The third time I tried to pay a Mexican taxi driver as he took me to a church: "No thank you. You are an Evangelical; so am I." And all three who made the refusal were not members of my race. And yet we discriminate against people like that.

Incidentally it may be said that a divine joke has been played on us. We have refused to call the Japanese citizens in our midst just plain Americans. We have called them Japanese—that is, Asiatics—and then to differentiate ourselves we have called ourselves "Caucasians." But the Caucasus is in Asia! So we have called ourselves Asiatics to distinguish ourselves from Asiatics!

The word "all" must mean "all"—or nothing.

7. *The seventh hesitation is in regard to applying the word "all" to all peoples beyond our own borders.* We hesitate to make this "all" attitude a universal principle. We forget that there is no such thing as local truth, for truth by its very nature is universal. Two and two make four

around the world—it is universal. But two and two make five—that is local. If democracy cannot be extended to all, it can be held by none. It is here that there is a central contradiction. We try to keep democracy at home and imperialism abroad—democracy for the white races and imperialism for colored races. But two thirds of the human race are colored and only one third is white. This means that the attitude of imperialism on the part of the white minority is bound to be bitterly resented by the colored majority. The first wave of resentment to hit the house of white imperialism is the Japanese assault. But it is only the first wave. Let us admit that Japanese imperialism is more brutal and harsh than white imperialism. But it is no more brutal and harsh than white imperialism was in its early stages. White imperialism had to learn by bitter experience that its methods and spirit had to soften to win the people under its control to any degree of tolerance. Japanese imperialism will learn the same lesson—is learning the same lesson. And if it does soften, it will have the inside track in the situation with its slogan, "Asia for the Asiatics."

There is one way and only one way for the white man to meet the situation in the lands where imperialisms hold sway, and that way is to renounce imperialism. It is entirely incompatible with democracy. You can have democracy or imperialism, but you cannot have both—they are incompatibles. Democracy and imperialism cannot exist in the same country without canceling out each other.

It is not enough to point to the benefits conferred by imperialism on subject peoples—roads, schools, hospitals, and a kind of peace. All of these benefits are canceled out in the minds of subject peoples by the fact of domination.

They want freedom—everybody does. It is inherent. A little Filipino boy taking an examination described the cow in the following terms: "A cow is an animal which stands on four legs fastened at the four corners. A cow gives milk, but as for me, give me liberty or give me death!" The little boy's outburst is in every human breast, everywhere around the world. Give a subject people everything except that one all-important thing, and you give them nothing.

When Jesus was hanging on the cross, they gave him drink in a sponge on a spearpoint. "They put a sponge . . . on a spear." (John 19:29—Moffatt.) Even their charities had the spearpoint of domination behind them. When we offer the sponges of benefit to subject peoples, remember that they feel the spearpoints of domination behind these sponges. The spearpoints enter their very souls. When Mahatma Gandhi was about to begin his civil disobedience movement back in 1921, I wrote to him and begged him not to do it. I felt it was too explosive, too dangerous. He wrote me in reply: "May I assure you that I shall not embark on civil disobedience without just cause, not without proper precautions, not without deep searchings of heart, and not without copious prayer. You have, perhaps, no notion of the wrong that this Government has done and is still doing to the vital part of our being. But I must not argue—I invite you to pray with and for me." "The wrong . . . to the vital part of our being"—that was the pressure of the spearpoint. Offer a man in that condition any number of sponges and they cannot atone for the pressure of the spearpoint of domination. There is one thing, and only one thing to do: withdraw the spearpoint.

The subject peoples of the world will spurn with increasing contempt all our sponges of benefit handed to them on the spearpoints of domination. Withdraw the spearpoints and they will take everything good with open-hearted gratitude.

India is the acid test of whether or not we intend to withdraw the spearpoints of imperialistic domination. Not ready for self-government? Exactly the same arguments made against India's demand for self-government were made against us in colonial days: "Too divided," "No experience in self-government," and "Someone else will get them." We *were* divided. "Fire and water," wrote Burnaby in 1760, after traveling more than a thousand miles in the Colonies, "are not more heterogeneous than the different colonies in North America." We were divided, but we took the risks of freedom and have become one of the most united peoples on earth. India has the same right to take the risks of freedom. The Hindus and Moslems would come to agreement, I believe, if they sat down face to face with no third party to whom each could appeal against the other. Suppose the worst came to worst and there should be civil war; would that be any worse than what has happened in Britain and America before these countries attained inner unity? Are we the only ones who have a right to civil wars if we want them? Besides, we who have spent fifty per cent of our time in war during our European history and have produced two world wars in one generation have earned no right to preach peace to peace-loving India and China. We who have dragged India into two world wars now piously say, "We cannot let you take the risks of freedom, lest there be internal conflict." At least India would not fight anyone except herself. I believe she would settle her differences without war.

But does India now have "peace"? With tens of thousands of her leaders in jail and the whole country a suppressed but seething volcano? And why are those leaders in jail? For asking for the thing that the Allied Nations are supposed to be fighting for!

In the meantime two thirds of the human race are looking on, and they are getting our answer—the answer is India. Freedom is not for the colored man; it is only for the white man. India is the place where this whole matter of freedom impinges upon a colored race. Freedom has been given to the white portions of the Commonwealth—Canada, Australia, New Zealand, South Africa—will it be given to the colored people? The answer is what we do with India. If that answer is hesitant and a giving of grudging concessions, then the colored races have the answer: they are on one side and the white races are on the other. If that happens, then we must accommodate ourselves to the fact of an inevitable clash between the one-third white minority and the two-thirds colored majority. That clash would make this one seem like a tempest in a teapot. But that clash is not inevitable; it can be headed off, and headed off by bridging the gap between the colored and the white at the place of India? How?

Let imperialism be renounced. Let all portions of all empires capable of immediate self-government be given it at once, or a definite date set for the beginning of self-government. Let their freedom be guaranteed by Britain, Russia, America, and China. To have China guarantee their freedom is important; it will be an Asiatic nation guaranteeing the freedom of Asiatic nations. Let the rest be put into the hands of an international body, pledged to bring them self-government at the earliest possible date. Let the gateways of the world be internationalized: Gibraltar, Suez, Singapore, and Panama. That will let down world tensions, for these world tensions arise out of jealousies between those who "have" and those who "have not."

Philosophies of aggression are built up by the "have not" nations to justify the breaking up of the *status quo*. That *status quo* will be broken up by consent or by force. We call those who try to break the *status quo* "aggressors." They are. But are not those who refuse to change an unjust *status quo* also aggressors? Both are aggressors. An unjust *status quo* must be broken up by consent—by the renunciation of imperialism. "The only way to beat them is to beat them to it." Let the democracies slough off this anachronism of imperialism and be themselves. They will be happier, and they will be more prosperous. For colonies don't pay. The nations that have them spend more than they are worth in keeping up huge military establishments to protect them, and then render themselves hopelessly in debt in paying for wars precipitated over colonies, symbols of ascendency in the world. Great Britain reduced to the homogeneous parts of the Commonwealth—Canada, Australia, New Zealand, South Africa—would be unified within, would excite no jealousy, would speak on democracy and freedom with moral authority, could lead us. But Great Britain holding on to one fourth of the land space of the world, and with a tremendous temptation to add to it at the close of this war, is an inward contradiction.

Just as there are two Americas—the America of freedom

and democracy and the America that would deny that freedom and democracy to the colored races—so there are two Britains. There is the Britain of democracy, the lover of liberty, the mother of Parliaments, the creator of the Commonwealth. But there is another Britain—the Britain of empire. This Britain of empire works behind the moral shield of the Britain of democracy, and always in its own interest. With the Britain of democracy we can go anywhere. With the Britain of empire we cannot go unless we are prepared to go to war every twenty-five years to rescue imperialisms under the guise of rescuing democracies. In the final showdown, after the wars reveal the ends in view, we find to our dismay that we have rescued imperialisms instead of democracies. It is the last time the American people can be induced to rescue decaying imperialisms from the wars into which imperialisms by their very nature periodically plunge them. There is one way out: renounce imperialism!

And that means American imperialism as well. For I have no desire to substitute American imperialism—economic or political—or a combination of American and British imperialism for British or any other imperialism. That would be just as dangerous as British imperialism. And we will be hated in the same way and rightly so. Those who talk about "the American century" are pushing this country down the slippery road of imperialism and its inevitable wars. If we take that path, we will renounce our birthright of democracy for a mess of imperialistic pottage.

Let America be anchored to her words "all men," and let her world mission be the implementing of those words in world affairs. Let her become "the servant of all." Then according to her Master, by that very service she will become the greatest of all. She will rise to the top like cream—and ought to! For then her rise will be beneficent to all. But the catch is in that phrase "servant of *all*." If you are the servant of some—white people, people of a certain class or race—then you do not become great, except a great snob. The moral universe is inexorable: if you save your life you lose it, it decays; but if you lose your life in service to others you find it again—it comes back to you built up and authoritative.

The future of the world is in the hands of those who will best serve the world. If the brown races, the yellow races, or the black races serve the world better than the white races, they will rise to leadership—and ought to! America has the formula: "All men are created equal, . . . endowed by their Creator with certain unalienable Rights." Let her translate that formula into fact and her future is assured. Let her world mission be: Equality of opportunity to "all men," everywhere! Then the suppressed and exploited peoples of the earth will lift up their heads in hope, and our own hearts will have within them a song—a song of freedom. And our youth will have a cause—the cause of world freedom.

Then our seven hesitations with the word "all" will be over; we will be all-out for freedom, for all men, in all the world. A power economy will come to an end, and a welfare economy begin.

Chapter V—

THE SEVEN HESITATIONS OF AMERICAN CHRISTIANITY

IF AMERICAN DEMOCRACY has been wrestling with something bigger than itself—that word "all"—then American Christianity has also been wrestling with something bigger than itself—the Christianity of Christ. Just as we have not been able to give up the word "all," nor give up to it, so we have not been able to give up the Christianity of Christ, nor give up to it.

The Christianity of Christ is a Person embodying a Kingdom. As such it is completely totalitarian. It demands a total allegiance in the total life. In turn it offers redemption and harmony and fulfillment to the total life.

H. G. Wells says: "The Galilean has been too great for our small hearts." He has been. And moreover the Christianity of Christ has been too big for our various small Christianities, including American Christianity. This Christianity has had seven great hesitations.

1. *It has hesitated to apply the power of the Christian faith to the body.* It has turned over the matter of physical health to the doctors and psychiatrists on the one hand, or has allowed it to drift into the hands of the marginal cults on the other. Physical health has not been a serious concern of the main stream of American Christianity. The

power of the Christian faith has not been made available for bodily health to the ordinary, regular member of our churches. He looks on it as something foreign to the faith he holds. And this in spite of the fact that his own Master spent a large part of his time and emphasis and power on the bodily health of those around him. It was an integral part of his mission.

It is now clear that you can pass on the sicknesses of the body to the mind and to the soul, and likewise that you can pass on the sicknesses of the mind and the soul to the body. Medical opinion is now prepared to say that fully fifty per cent of bodily ills do not originate in the body, but in the mind and soul. If that is true, then the Christian Church can no longer concern itself solely with the so-called "spiritual" and give no concern to the physical; for body, mind, and soul are bound up in one bundle of life. But American Christianity has hesitated to apply the implications of its teachings to physical health. I return to this discussion in a later chapter.

2. *The second hesitation is in regard to another area—the mind.* The Church has only too often been afraid to allow men to think, and to think freely. This fear has arisen out of the fact that the Christian faith is supposed to be written in the Bible alone and not written into the constitution of the universe as well. If we believe that the Christian faith is written into the structure of reality, as well as in the pages of Scripture, then we will not only allow men to think freely but will urge them to do so. For the facts, wherever discovered, will bring men out to the same place —at the fact of Christ.

This hesitation on the part of American Christianity is

vividly seen in the words of the governor of Virginia in 1671: "I thank God we have no free schools nor printing; and I hope we shall not have these hundred years. For learning has brought disobedience and heresy and sects into the world; and printing has divulged them and libels against the Government. God keep us from both." We have outgrown this in large measure, but as yet we have not come up to the statement of Jesus: "Thou shalt love the Lord thy God . . . with *all* thy mind." The whole mind free to explore the whole universe—unafraid! Unafraid, because it knows that "without him [Christ] was not anything made that was made," and that his touch is upon everything and everything leads ultimately to him.

3. *The third hesitation has been to apply the Christian faith to labor and industry.* A working agreement has been tacitly entered into between the Church and industry—the Church is to have Sundays and industry the rest of the week. "Business is business," and "there should be no mixing of religion and business." Business will pay the bills provided the Church keeps to its own preserves and lets business alone. It is seldom stated that baldly, but the Church is often under the domination of that thought. One hesitates to say, with someone, that "the Church has often been the kept mistress of industry," but I'm afraid that this has often been dangerously near the truth. One prominent minister who was to speak before a national convention of businessmen submitted his address to the local group to see if it met their approval. He "took the money, and did as he was taught."

The Church has on the whole allied itself to the upper middle classes and has for the most part lost contact with labor, especially organized labor. The reason for this apparently has been the subconscious feeling that if the Church is in close contact with labor it may offend the leaders of industry in the Church, for industry has only grudgingly recognized organized labor. The Church has for the most part reflected that attitude. I was about to speak to an audience of about four thousand people in an Eastern city. Three persons arose to interpret the needs of that audience: a minister told what the ministers needed, a businessman what the businessmen needed, a student the needs of youth. "Now," said the chairman, "you have had the needs of this audience interpreted to you; speak to those needs." I was deeply moved. Here was a method that would keep the minister close to life; it might be tried on Sunday mornings! It was a grand method. But I was also shocked—shocked that the Christian Church could visualize the needs of that audience and leave out labor, and could do it unconsciously. It showed vividly where the Christian Church is set in American society—the upper middle classes. It has lost touch with labor. This is serious; for if labor is allowed to drift away from the Christian faith, then with the masses of labor paganized, industry is a dog-eat-dog affair—selfishness ruling both capital and labor.

When we began the National Christian Mission it was with the greatest difficulty that I could get in touch with the leaders of labor in the different cities. I became almost a gadfly in the situation in my insistence that we must try to Christianize organized labor. And then I saw the reason: the local church leaders were for the most part not in touch with organized labor, and hence could not get me in touch with them. In later Missions the problem was solved by nationally known Christian leaders' going about with us to relate our Mission to local labor. The lack of vital touch with organized labor on the part of American Christianity is nothing short of tragic. American labor need not go anti-Christian as European labor has gone. It is approachable and responsive. "We do not want to go anti-Christian," said a labor leader to me; "we simply thought the Church didn't care." The Church must care if it continues to be Christian.

When Philip Murray, the head of the most radical group of organized labor, could say these words, then America has nothing to fear from organized labor and everything to hope for: "Labor must think in terms beyond itself—it must think for the good of the whole. So capital must think in terms beyond itself—it must think in terms of the good of the whole. When we both do that, then we will make real progress." When the head of the C.I.O. can say that, then the door is open for the Christian spirit to guide the labor movement.

If there is hope regarding labor leaders, there is also hope regarding supposedly conservative Christian bodies. A commission of Episcopalians, headed by a bishop, makes this declaration: "The economic order exists to serve God by increasing the welfare of man." It challenges our present economic order because of "its distortion of true values through exaggerated acquisitiveness," because of "its indefensible inequalities of opportunity," the "tyranny of our concentration of irresponsible economic power," and "the wickedness of a system which prevents most men from finding a sense of Christian vocation in their daily life." It further adds: "We believe the idea that by pursuing individual interests there would be created a universal harmony of interests which would serve the good of all is no longer adequate. . . . The human being is primary; . . . to make the 'profit rule' the directive force and predominant factor in industry is an improper reversal of values." This commission says that unemployment is "the final curse of any social system. Unemployment is cured in time of war; it can also be cured in time of peace. . . . The whole people, acting through its government, should assume responsibility for the elimination of unemployment." It further recommends "employee participation in management" and "social insurance."

When a branch of the Christian Church, made up in large measure of conservative economic interests, can speak in these terms, and when labor can speak in the terms of Philip Murray as quoted above, then the future holds hope. Our economic life might be Christianized.

Certainly the appalling hesitation on the part of a large part of the Christian Church to apply the Christian faith to industry and labor should be at an end.

4. *The fourth hesitation is the hesitation to apply the Christian faith to the question of race.* There is the saying that "beauty is only skin deep," and yet there has been nothing deeper than skin—at least nothing deeper in our prejudices. And nothing so absurd! What could be more absurd than this: A Negro youth had a real talent for composing music and wrote the composition used by the high-school band at the commencement exercises. But the composer sat in the upper gallery, segregated, and couldn't even come to the platform to receive his diploma. And this is not in the deep South, for there he would not have been allowed

even to attend a white school, but in Kansas City. Another absurdity: A Negro basketball player really won the state championship for his high school. A "victory dance" in celebration was arranged, and when this youth and his colored partner arrived to participate in the dance he was politely told to leave. "Only skin deep?" There is nothing deeper than skin! And yet when we look at it we find there is nothing deep about skin except prejudices. And these are removable!

The Christian Church could remove those prejudices were it true to itself. Race prejudice was transcended in the early Church. Paul and Barnabas were called of the Holy Spirit to go out from Antioch on a tour of evangelism which brought them to Europe. But in going out they were ordained by a Negro among others. A Negro's hands were laid on Paul and Barnabas to ordain them to preach the gospel to white Europe. "Now there were in the church that was at Antioch certain prophets and teachers; as Barnabas, and Simeon that was called Niger, and Lucius of Cyrene, and Manaen, which had been brought up with Herod the tetrarch, and Saul. . . . When they had . . . laid their hands on them, they sent them away." (Acts 13:1, 3.) The word "Niger" is literally "the Black," the word from which our word "Negro" comes. The black man in the early Church was not on the edges but centrally and fundamentally one of the fellowship in position and authority. And among them was "Manaen," a foster brother of Herod the tetrarch—a man high up in society—and yet Simeon was in that group, naturally and normally. That was the position of the man of color in the early Church.

To see the apostasy of our Christianity note this: A

church was organized in Pasadena, California, called "The Fellowship Church (Interracial)," its membership made up of all churches—a church within the Church, to meet once a month on Sunday afternoon. I was invited to speak to the two thousand people present at its opening. I said, "This is both a triumph and a tragedy—a triumph in that you have at last come to a place in the Christian Church where race distinctions are blotted out, but a tragedy in that after two thousand years of wandering you arrive at the place where the Christian Church began."

The Christian Church in America has apostatized, and instead of being a voice it has become an echo. Instead of creating its own society, no matter what the surrounding society might be, it has simply reflected that society. The spirit of surrounding culture has invaded the Christian Church and has made us into its own image. We reflect its race prejudices. And yet the world expects the Church to be different. A gentleman took his Negro chauffeur into a Y.W.C.A. restaurant, and they sat down together and ate. A white patron got up from another seat, went to the cashier and said, "Do you allow that Negro to eat here?" "Yes," she replied, "we are for everybody." He went back to his seat. After a while he got up and went back to the cashier and said, "You're right. I am glad the Y.W. is taking this position and is for everybody."

Albert Schweitzer says, "When collectivity influences the individual more than the individual influences it, then decline sets in." That could be put this way: When surrounding culture influences the Christian Church more than the Christian Church influences surrounding culture, then decay sets in. We must cease our hesitations and work out from our principles to collective life, and not allow collective life to work from its lack of principles in to us and invade us with its prejudices and its consequent confusions. We must be not an echo but a voice; we must act and not merely react.

5. *The fifth hesitation of American Christianity is in regard to the application of Christian principles and spirit to domestic politics and foreign relations.* As a consequence of this hesitation the political life of America is generally below the level of the life of the people. American life in general is higher than its political life.

The financial rewards of business have been so much higher than the financial rewards of honest politics that the best brains and talent of this country has been drained off from the political life into business. The political life has been impoverished, morally and intellectually. The great cities of America are, with fine exceptions, in the hands of a low type of boss-ridden political machine. And they are this way because the Christian Church allows them to be this way. The Christian Church with its sixty-five million membership holds the balance of power in this country. If it knew how to think and act together, it could throw the balance of power any way it chose. For it has the largest single allegiance, around a common loyalty, of any group in American life.

But it has allowed the political life of America to get into other than Christian hands. And one of the things that is responsible for this situation is the wedge that has been driven between the secular and the sacred. Christianity has to do with the sacred, the spiritual; and the secular, the material, is turned over into whatever hands may be able to grasp and control it. This has been the great Christian abdication. Instead of inspiring its youth to choose political careers, and instead of insisting that its more mature members go into politics, it has tacitly approved of their staying out, for "politics is a dirty business." It is, and the neglect of the Christian Church has made it so.

This neglect of domestic politics has led to the neglect of foreign relations. The Church has largely confined its foreign relations to Christian missions and social service. Good, but not good enough. For a pagan decision on the part of our government may cancel out all we have tried to do through missions and social service.

In two outstanding situations in our history we have allowed a local sectional outlook to determine a national policy and thus get the nation as a nation into trouble. The year 1876 marked the end of the tragic "carpetbag government" era. It had to end for it was wrong. But that same year marked the beginning of another wrong. In order to try to heal the breach between North and South, we turned over the question of the Negro to be determined locally by the South. What was an essentially national question we delivered into the hands of local prejudices to be dealt with locally. When that was done, the Negro was disfranchised by various expedients, and emancipation was arrested and ceased to be emancipation. Result? The nation gets the blame for our treatment of the Negro. Throughout the world it is a black mark against us. The Church, the one detached body, could have prevented this. But it was an echo, instead of a voice.

Again, we allowed local race prejudices against people from Asia and vested interests on the West Coast to determine the foreign policy of the national government and through it to embitter the whole of the East against us. As a Christian missionary I have had to explain to the East that our government is not Christian and cannot therefore be expected to act in a Christian way. But that is an explanation that doesn't explain. Why isn't the government Christian in its foreign policies? It isn't because the Christian Church has never said it should be. It has abdicated where it should have admonished and advised and directed. Foreign affairs have been foreign to the Christian Church. This must cease if the Christian Church isn't to cease—as a potent force for regeneration.

6. *The sixth hesitation on the part of American Christianity has been, and still is, in regard to the application of Christian principles to war.* It has in large measure adopted prevailing attitudes instead of keeping its own. It has its own. How anyone can fit war in with the spirit of Jesus Christ is an enigma. The early Christian conscience completely repudiated war. For the first three centuries no Christian ever went to war. Then the great decay of conscience began. And that decay is still with us.

And yet there is hope. There is one difference between this and other wars: nobody believes in this one! Even those who feel that they must support it know that this isn't the way. Their attitude is: "Well, we're caught in it, and we must go through with it, but, this isn't the way." I have repeated this statement before large audiences across the country, and not one person has ever come up to me at the close to challenge it. Even in the midst of war with its vast propaganda for support of it something has happened to the mind of America. That is sheer gain. A Republican leaders' group recently put out a statement saying that we must plan to get rid of war, and in today's paper Mr. Hull speaks of "the monstrous specter of war." If this can take place when war is on, what will the kickback be when the aftermath of war with its disillusionments begins fully to register? I predict that the greatest revulsion against war that the world has ever seen will then take place.

Will the Church lead that revolt? In spite of the decay in the older generation of Christians in falling away to war pressures, I still think it will. For the younger generation is sounder. It is giving its material support to war but is withholding its moral support. It goes into it, but with no enthusiasm, no waving of banners, and no singing. This is not a singing war. Why? There is no inner moral approval of it. It is a mess to be cleaned up, instead of a message to be proclaimed.

Someone was talking to a group of fifty-four high-school students. When the group was asked how many would refuse to support the war, only one hand went up. When asked how many wished they had enough Christlikeness to refuse to support the war, twenty-seven hands went up. When asked how many believed that Jesus Christ would participate in war, only one hand went up. If that is any index of what is happening in the soul of youth, then we have hope. But we have no hope whatever from the type of Christianity that hesitates to apply its Christian principles in regard to war when war is on. If it waits to ride on the bandwagon of disillusionment and revolt against war when war is over, then it has forfeited its right to lead.

7. *The seventh hesitation on the part of American Chris-*

101

LINCOLN BIBLE INSTITUTE

tianity is to give sufficient approval of varying types of denominational expression to be able to work together as a unit. We have come a long way from the hanging of Quakers in Boston because they differed from the prevailing type, but we still have our hesitations, many of them only inwardly expressed. We are seldom as frank as the clerk of the church in Burlington, Vermont, who wrote in the church register in the early days: "We thank God we have a church bell 741 pounds heavier than any church bell in town." Nevertheless there are suppressed rivalries and many hesitations.

These hesitations should come to an end. The idea that any partciular denomination is the exclusive, or even particular, channel of God's grace is as dead as Queen Anne. And she is very dead! God killed the idea, or let it die from neglect; for he seems to use persons, not because of where they are denominationally located, but because of their depth of surrender to him. God sometimes works through the denomination, sometimes in spite of it, but never exclusively or particularly in any one of them. If that hurts your denominational pride, it may help your Christian humility!

In a divided world seeking unity a divided Church not seeking unity has little or no moral authority. But it must more than seek unity; it must achieve unity. How that unity might be achieved we will discuss later. The next great step in American Christianity is to get together. Its moral leadership in American life and in world life depends on it.

We have analyzed, briefly, the seven hesitations of American democracy and the seven hesitations of American Christianity. Can these hesitations be brought to an end, and can both democracy and Christianity work together and yet be really themselves without hesitations and without reservations? If so, how?

Chapter VI

THE CENTRAL GENIUS OF AMERICAN DEMOCRACY

WE HAVE SEEN the contradictions in American democracy. Those contradictions are not so much a fundamental disbelief in the principles of democracy but a hesitation to apply those principles in every area of life at home and abroad. We have hold of something bigger than our expression of it.

What are we to do with a people thus hesitant and divided against itself? Are we mentally to throw them overboard and look for a more perfect instrument of the purposes of God in this world crisis? Where could we find it? Scandinavia might be that instrument, for her mentality is set in the right direction. Given another ten years Scandinavia might have shown the way out without revolution. She was distributing her wealth widely through co-operatives. The future flag of the world will probably be patterned after Denmark's—red with a white cross on it, the red of humanity with the cross of redemptive divinity. But Scandinavia lacks the material resources to make herself decisive in world affairs. The same with Switzerland. Britain might be that instrument if she should decide to reduce herself to the Commonwealth—Canada, Australia, New Zealand, South Africa—a homogeneous group, a group that would excite no jealousy but would evoke only admiration and love. That Britain we could love—wholeheartedly. But the Britain of empire, attached to the Britain of democracy, is the incubus which unfits Britain to be the instrument of God in this world crisis. For the world is not sure which Britain is speaking— the Britain of democracy or the Britain of empire. Empire by its very nature is bound to work in its own interests, and always in its own interests. Some years ago I asked a British officer in charge of the air defense of the Persian Gulf how it happened that they had allowed the Americans to come in and take the oil at Bahrein, on the Persian Gulf, right out from under Britain's nose? To which he replied: "For once in our lives we were clever. We knew if we allowed America to have this oil we could rely on her to come and defend it and thus help us defend the Persian Gulf." Our soldiers are now at Karachi, India, opposite Bahrein! It cannot be said that the real reason for their being there is to defend that oil, but it is one of the reasons. The prophecy of the British officer has come true.

No, the road of empire is too slippery—slippery down the road to perpetual wars. Britain might be the instrument of God for world reconstruction if she would renounce empire for democracy, but with Mr. Churchill, the apostle of empire, at the helm there is little likelihood of her doing so. She will probably continue to be two Britains canceling each other out.

China might, someday, be the instrument of that world peace, but not now. She is too weak, and not yet internally reconstructed and regenerated. She has the mentality, and the material resources to work with, but has a great cultural and spiritual lag to make up. India might do it, but she is a subject people, and she has not yet found her soul. She too has the mentality for peace, but not the open opportunity to apply it. A Hindu once said to me: "We Hindus should exchange sacred books with you Christians of the West. Our sacred book, the Bhagawad Gita, teaches war; and your sacred book, the New Testament, teaches peace. We should exchange sacred books; it would suit us both better."

It all sifts down to Russia and America as the possibilities for reconstruction. Russia, up to the time of the attack on Finland, had given hopes that she was not imperialistic. Her attack on Finland lost for her moral ground in the East; Russia too is imperialistic, was the reaction. It was a disastrous step, and will be heavily paid for; it will be atoned for with difficulty. Russia may make that atonement. Her offer of freedom to the sixteen constituent elements of the U. S. S. R. and her announcement that she cannot deal with the Polish Government in Exile because it is "imperialistic" may be the announcement of an intention—she will not be imperialistic. If so, then a large part of Europe and a large part of Asia may gravitate toward her. Russia has the seeds of democracy within her. Russians said this to me again and again while I was there: "We are the inheritors of democracy. You began it and then grew afraid of it. You tried to confine it to the political. We took it and applied it to the social and economic. So we took the torch from your hand."

The answer to that cannot be a verbal retort; it must be a vital reply—a demonstration. I think America can give that demonstration. Democracy is more interwoven with the texture of her life and more inherent in her faith than in that of Russia. Therefore I feel that God, and we, are shut up to America, with all her faults, as probably the best available instrument of God for this hour.

Amid all the contradictions in American life there shine three hopeful things: (1) *a ruling concept,* faith in man, based on a faith in God; (2) *a central expression of its genius, "E pluribus unum";* (3) *a cleansing principle and power working within her life,* Christ. Add to these three things the background of the fact that we have no real desire for world domination, and no real desire for territorial expansion; then there is hope for the world in these three things.

The first and last of these three things are absent in Russia. Her faith in man is based on a humanism and is not supported by a moral universe. Her faith in man therefore cannot last unless she gets a larger faith. Nor has she the cleansing principle and power of Christ working in her life; she has had to depend on blood purges. She does have *"E pluribus unum,"* but not with the same depth as America and not with the same rootage in her national history.

"E pluribus unum"—"Out of the many one"—is woven into the texture of our national life; in fact it is the central genius of that national life. It will probably be our greatest gift to the world. For in this principle we have discovered a universal principle.

I cannot account for our fastening on this principle except through divine guidance. We could easily have missed it, in fact came near doing so. Only about ten men saw the vision of a federal union—out of the many one. We came near taking the way the League of Nations tried. We considered seriously a "League of Friendship" which would attempt to bind together sovereign colonies. Had we done that we should have failed exactly as the League of Nations failed. The League of Nations was trying to have a world brotherhood without any surrender of national sovereignty. Each nation within the League retained its sovereignty intact; every decision had to be unanimous. Every nation refused to surrender itself to a union of the whole. They saved their lives, and they lost them. They ran against that law of the Kingdom deeply imbedded in the moral universe: "Whosoever will save his life shall lose it: and whosoever will lose his life . . . shall find it." The only possible way to find life is to lose it in something higher than itself; then it comes back again. But center yourself on yourself and make yourself sovereign, and that self will go to pieces. That is true of the individual, and it is true of the group or nation. If America had gone into the League, the result would have been the same. Its life might have been prolonged a bit, but in the end the result would have been the same collapse. The League broke itself upon the moral universe. If a group of archangels had constituted the League, the result would have been precisely the same. The League was trying the impossible. You simply cannot have a union without surrender of some sovereignty to that union.

Suppose a husband and a wife should decide that neither one would surrender any individual sovereignty to the union, what would be the result? There would be no union! The probabilities are that there would be a breakdown in a divorce court. The relationship would break itself on a universal law.

Had the Colonies taken the "League of Friendship" it would have broken to pieces under the strain of sovereign colonial self-interest, and we would have had another Europe on our hands—forty-eight sovereign states with tariffs and duties and passports and armaments and perpetual wars. But we decided to do the impossible thing, to lose colonial sovereignty in a union. The great renunciation was made. The Colonies lost themselves and found themselves in the most complete and lasting union of the world.

In forming a federal union they not only obeyed a law of the moral universe; they also obeyed a law written in themselves. There are two great instincts within man: a desire for union with the whole and a desire for freedom. They seem incompatible. But really, if properly related, they are not only compossibles but affinities. The only way to find freedom is to obey something higher than yourself. Then you gain individual local freedom within that sovereignty.

The Colonies decided, not to form a federation which would have left the sovereignty of the constituent elements intact, but to form a federal *union* in which individual sovereignty was lost in a higher sovereignty—sovereignty of the union. That satisfied the desire for union with the whole. Then they decided to give local self-government within the states. Under the supreme sovereignty of the union the states were free to express their state life as they saw fit. They had union, and they had freedom. But how did they have freedom when they pledged themselves to obey something beyond themselves? They found freedom in obeying that union, for that union was themselves. Its decisions were their decisions. The union was themselves acting in a corporate capacity.

They took the sovereignty of this union with hesitation.

In the original draft of the Constitution the words "the United States" were written "the united States"; the word "united" was an adjective modifying the proper noun "States." The states loomed large, and the union was small. But now this has been reversed: the word "United" is no longer an adjective; it is a very proper noun and getting more proper every day! The union is supreme, and while we have our local state loyalties, yet our highest loyalty, politically speaking, is to the "The United States."

In choosing federal union we avoided two pitfalls: the pitfall of having complete sovereignty in each state, and the pitfall of having complete sovereignty in the union. The first would have produced the counterpart of the anarchistic modern sovereign nation, responsible to nothing except itself, and the second would have produced the modern totalitarian government. We balanced them and found a federal union—the most solidly based of all unions, for it is founded upon the fulfillment of the two deep instincts in our nation, the desire for union and the desire for freedom. I am persuaded that nothing but divine guidance could have guided us to that. We discovered an ultimate principle in government. The future of the world may be shaped by it.

Europe took the opposite and adopted *"E pluribus multum"*—"Out of the many, many"—and in the last "many" she has included many wars, and will continue to include many wars until she decides on the *"E pluribus unum."* Then her wars will cease, and we will cease being dragged into them. For the real war which Europe is waging is with the Kingdom of God, which says, "Whosoever will save his life shall lose it." All her lesser wars are symptoms of that central war.

America obeyed that law, and to that degree the moral universe has been behind her. *"E pluribus unum"* is her central genius, and will probably be her central contribution to the world.

Chapter VII

THE THREEFOLD GENIUS OF THE CHRISTIAN FAITH

THE CHRISTIAN FAITH creates faith in man through faith in God who created man. But that faith in man could not be sustained unless there were a continuous principle and power in the person of Christ to re-create man. Nor could it be sustained unless that faith were a reconciling power to unite men on a higher level in a human brotherhood. The threefold genius of the Christian faith is that: (1) it creates faith in God which creates faith in men; (2) it re-creates men; and (3) it reconciles and unites men.

There is nothing so necessary in a democracy as a continuous faith in man in spite of his weaknesses and his failures. But that faith cannot be sustained on a humanistic level. You cannot long believe in man unless you believe in something more than man—something which gives him permanence and ultimate meaning. I saw an atheistic funeral in Russia—the funeral of a child. Not only was the child dead: the funeral ceremonies were dead; they had no lift nor life in them; the parents could not sing in that hour, for hope was buried with the child. When there is no permanent meaning to life after death there is no permanent meaning to life before death. Life is devaluated.

I was talking to Dr. George Carver, the Negro saint and

scientist, a man who contributed an estimated $75,000,000 to the agriculture of the South by discovering from the lowly sweet potato 150 commercial products and from the peanut 300 commercial products. I told him of a chemist who had said to me that life was only the result of a combination of chemical elements like the flame that comes from combustion, that when the chemical elements disintegrated life disintegrated with it, and there was nothing more to it. I asked what he, as a chemist, would reply to the other chemist. His reply was a shaking of the head and the words: "The poor man—the poor man!" And that *was* the reply. The other man was a poor man in comparison with Carver; he was impoverished by a poor faith—a faith that cheapened life and made it ultimately worthless.

Put those two faiths under life and see the ultimate results. Carver's faith produced Carver. But it did more than produce Carver; it produced faith in millions of Negroes beaten by poverty and social suppressions. It made them lift their heads. I asked Dr. Carver how he ever got started in his marvelous discoveries, and his reply was: "I took a peanut and put it in my open hand and said, 'Mr. Creator, what's in that peanut?' and the Creator answered and said, 'You have brains, go and find out.'" A lovely answer for a Creator to give! Dr. Carver did more than discover possibilities in peanuts; he discovered possibilities in people—himself the chief demonstraton. A man who was sold as a slave boy for a broken-down race horse became one of America's greatest citizens and contributors, honored by a grateful country.

A nation that has within it a faith that produces an outstanding chemist out of a slave boy—a somebody out of a nobody—has within it a hope-giving principle. A saving, stimulating power is working at its heart.

When I stood in a certain pulpit and I opened the large Bible, the pulpit light shining upon its pages lighted up my face; when I closed the Bible, my face was dark. As long as America has an open Bible, the face of the American man will be lighted up; when that Bible is closed, then the light will die from the face of the American man. Democracy gets its light and inspiration from the Eternal Word.

Harry Lauder said: "I could tell where the lamplighter was by the trail of light left behind him." You can tell where the Christ of the American Road has been by the trail of lighted lives he has left behind him.

But this Christ has not only enlightened men's lives. He has enlivened them. He has introduced into life a cleansing, regenerating power that quickens conscience, gives moral power, and makes men care—makes them care what happens to others—it sensitizes them. "It's not on my body," is the phrase that was responsible for China's downfall. It is the phrase that, with a shrug of the shoulders, threw off all social responsibility. China had sunk so low that one of its patriots, Dr. Chang Po-ling, was in such despair that he formed a Suicides' Pact—a group of patriots who would commit collective suicide to try to shock the country into doing something for China's regeneration. It was a counsel of despair, but it was the best they knew. Before Chang Po-ling's Suicides' Pact could be operative he happened to get hold of a New Testament. It struck him with surprise. Here was teaching and power in one; it was not a set of dead precepts like his Confucian ethics, but a power to make bad men into good men, hopeless men into radiantly hopeful men, the negative, beaten man into the positive, creative man. He opened his heart to it. The power of Christ came into him and transformed him. Instead of dying for China he would live for China. He has—amazingly. He set up the wonderful Nankai University at Tientsin, filled with the new, hopeful China. As soon as the war began, the Japanese bombed it straight off; that was the way to destroy China—destroy her hope-bringing institutions. A lesser spirit would have been beaten, but not Dr. Chang Po-ling, for he moved his university two thousand miles to Chungking. When the Japanese bombed this newly built plant also, he rebuilt. His son was killed as an aviator over Shanghai. But, nothing daunted, he goes straight on, unbeaten, unbeatable. It is because that spirit has been introduced into new China—the spirit that says, "It *is* on my body; it *is* my responsibility"— that China stands the staggering blows rained upon her, and will emerge unbroken from this terrible ordeal. At the heart of China is a group of Christian leaders, and at the heart of those Christian leaders is working a regenerating principle and power in the person of Christ.

That same principle and power has been working at the heart of America. If it were not, there would be little hope in either country. As I stood in the early days of the Chinese Republic beside the beheading block in Canton, China, where the executioner had cut off the heads of thirty-five thousand people each with a single blow, I turned to my Chinese guide and said, "But you don't do this now, do you?" "Oh no," he said, his face lighting up, "we a republic; we hang 'em, all same as you." Without the Christian faith the difference between an autocracy and a democracy would be only the difference between beheading and hanging. But the Christian faith in America and in China says something else: "We regenerate 'em, all same as you." The difference between "regenerate" and "hang" is the difference between a country with a Christian faith and one without that faith; for if you don't regenerate men, you'll have to hang them. The Christian faith regenerates men and opens to them infinite possibilities. "Don't you know where Murphy is?" asked a lad. "That's where I live. You can get anywhere in the world from Murphy." You can! And you can take hold of Murphy the man—ordinary Irish clay, a clod—and with the power of Christ working at his heart, regenerating, inspiring him, that same Murphy can go places—he can go anywhere in the world. Faith in the common man is an essential necessity for democracy, and the Christian faith produces that faith.

If as someone has said, "we are unfinished masters of an unfinished world," then there is something—a Someone—working regeneratively to finish the unfinished masters and through them to help finish an unfinished world. Christ and his Kingdom are the answer to an unfinished man and an unfinished world.

But the Christian faith does something more than give faith in man and a power for his regeneration. It reconciles men on a higher level; it brings unity. If I were to put my finger on a verse that sums up the Christian faith better, perhaps, than any other, it would be this: "God was in Christ, reconciling the world unto himself, . . . and hath committed unto us the word of reconciliation." (II Cor. 5:19.) God was reconciling men to himself even when they did not want to be reconciled; the cross was the price God had to pay to get to men in spite of their sins. He took those sins and

116

made them his own, and thus bearing those sins on his own heart he came to men in reconciliation. He could forgive now, for the forgiveness would not be cheap—he had taken it all on himself. Reconciliation is the central, fundamental note of the Christian faith; and nothing, absolutely nothing, is more needed. For as long as man has the sense of being out of harmony with Reality, a dead hand is laid on him. Reconciliation lifts that dead hand, and instead stretches the hands of benediction over the reconciled soul.

If reconciliation is God's chief business, it is ours. He "hath committed unto us the word of reconciliation"; we are to carry on God's reconciling work. That is our chief work. We are to reconcile in three directions: between man and God, between man and himself, and between man and man. Our chief business is to make it possible for man to live with God, to live with himself, and to live with his fellows. These three hang together: if you will not live with God, then you cannot live with yourself, and you cannot live with others.

> Modern man is a lonely soul,
> Without a God and without a goal,
> Stumbling in the night
> Without a light,
> Barking his shins
> On the system of things,
> Hurting himself
> In the quest for pelf.
>
> The end of the story,
> Stark and without glory,
> Must be told in bitter prose.

117

For modern man is without repose;
The rhyme and rhythm have gone from life—
Man is plagued by inner strife.
The bitter prose is this:
He who would not live with God
Cannot live with himself.

E. S. J.

To live with ourselves and others we must learn to live with God. And then, and then only, can we live out our corporate lives.

The Christian faith must be a reconciling, unity-bringing power. How? By compromise? By appeasement? No, by reconciling men on a higher level by getting each to change. This verse, describing this possibility of reconciliation, became luminous to me at the beginning of the war, and has remained luminous, my chief guiding star amid the encircling gloom: "To make peace by the creation of a new Man in himself out of both parties." (Eph. 2:15—Moffatt.) The clash was between Jew and Gentile—each feeling he had a right to rule, the Jew because of a divine destiny and call, and the Roman Gentile because he had the imperialistic might. A man stepped into that situation who was eminently fitted to reconcile both, for he was a Jew and yet a Roman citizen. But more, he was a Christian, and as a Christian he got hold of a principle of reconciliation—a new principle. He saw that if Jew conquered Gentile there would be no peace; there would be only planned revenge; and if the Gentile conquered the Jew it would be the same. Conquest would be followed by revenge, and the whole thing would seesaw down through the warring years.

But there was a way to reconcile them: get them both to change, so that out of the two would emerge a new man; that new man would gather up the truth in each and eliminate the wrongs of each, so that they would be reconciled on a higher level; the creation of a new man out of both parties would make peace. It would make peace, for neither one would conquer the other, but something higher than each would conquer both. That would make peace, and that alone would make peace. Peace is not something concerning which you can say, "Now let's have peace." Peace cannot be had that way. Peace is a by-product of conditions out of which peace naturally comes.

Paul put his finger on a principle which is really a universal principle, and he could not have done it without divine inspiration. For this is a principle and a method which reaches from the simplest relationship to the most complex, from the personal to the international. In producing a person two cells lose themselves as separate entities and find themselves in a new man out of both parties. If either cell would refuse to surrender itself to a higher entity—the union of the two—then there would be no peace, only clash, and ultimately there would be no life. Peace comes through mutual surrender to a higher entity—the new man—and peace can come in no other way. This is basic. And it stretches from the cell to every relationship on earth—and in heaven.

I saw two children, good friends, come into a service. Each wanted to sit beside a favorite grown-up. One dodged past the other and triumphantly sat beside the grown-up; she had conquered. The other little girl had to take the seat in front. The first little girl was elated at the triumph of her pushing self-interest. But only for a moment, for she soon saw she had gained her way *at a price*. It was the price of fellowship. She had found herself, but she had lost her friend, and in doing so she discovered she had lost herself—she was unhappy, for the fellowship was broken. Then began a series of maneuvers to re-establish the fellowship. She tickled the back of her little friend's head, but the little friend paid no attention; she was hurt. Peace in that situation could be made in only one way: the one little girl must give up her selfish gain and go and sit with her friend, and then neither one would conquer the other, but love would conquer both, and out of the two a new person would arise. That new something which would have arisen would have been friendship, and friendship has been described as "two souls in one body."

Take a more fundamental relationship, the relationship between husband and wife. If either one tries to conquer the other, there will be no peace. If the husband tries to conquer the wife, knowing women as I do, I know there will be no peace! Or if the wife tries to conquer the husband, overtly or covertly, knowing men as I do, there will be no peace! There will be planned revenge, an attempt at getting ahead of the other. Moreover, even if there is no attempt to conquer the other, if there is only a refusal inwardly to surrender to the other, no love will spring up, for mutual self-surrender is the essence of love. There is only one way to a real love and consequently to peace: both must surrender to an entity higher than themselves, and then out of both parties will arise the new man, a love partnership. That and that alone lays the solid foundation of peace. Try in every other possible way to have peace, and you won't have it, for the universe won't back it. The universe backs this way and only this way. This is central in the Christian faith, and it is central in the universe.

William Hard in *Reader's Digest,* December, 1943, says we must have a "World Union," but must have no surrender of sovereignty to that "union." He' has chosen the wrong word; you can have a federation without losing sovereignty, but you can't have union. He has tacked the word "union" on to separate, sovereign entities, and it doesn't fit.

We have seen that the American democracy discovered the same principle and that the center of its genius became *"E pluribus unum"*—"Out of the many one"—a new man out of both parties. Our democracy made peace between the states, not by one portion's trying to rule the other portion, but by all the states' surrendering to something beyond themselves, the union; and thus out of all the states arose the new man, the United States of America. That has made peace. That peace was broken when the industrial North tried to control the planting South, and the planting South tried to control the industrial North. The issue of slavery was a concomitant issue; the central issue was a clash of sectional interests for control and dominance. And there was no peace; war was upon us, inevitably. The conditions for peace had been broken, the new man had become two men, and war resulted.

There can be peace in this land of ours as long as, and only as long as, no person, group, state, or section tries to conquer and control the others, but each person, group, state, and section is surrendered to something beyond itself —the good of the whole—the new man—America.

Before we go on to the application of this principle to

our total life we pause to note this important fact: Our Christian faith in its doctrine of the new man out of both parties and our democracy in its doctrine of *"E pluribus unum"*—"Out of the many one"—coincide in their essential outlook, purposes, and goal. The Christian faith and democracy, each true to itself, can be true to each other. They can and should work for the same ends. That is important, for suppose our faith and our democracy were essentially at cross purposes. That would throw confusion and conflict into our souls. It would make us a house divided against itself, and that house could not stand.

Now, as a Christian, and as an American, I can work for the production of a cleansed and united America and for a cleansed and united world, knowing that in doing so I have the united support of my faith and of my democracy.

When we were trying to head off this war with Japan, I called on the Australian Minister regarding the question of giving New Guinea to Japan as a place for her surplus population. "Have you raised this with your State Department?" he asked. "Yes, I have, but their reaction was that they couldn't raise it with you. They couldn't raise the question of giving away someone else's territory. So I'm the unofficial fool who rushes in where angels fear to tread." "Well, I suppose," he thoughtfully replied, "your business in life is that of a catalyst in chemistry—an agent that precipitates action in others but is itself unaffected." "Good!" I replied to myself. "That is exactly what a Christian should be; he should be the friend of all and get everybody to change and be reconciled on a higher level." The chief business of the Christian is reconciliation by producing in every situation a new man out of both parties.

Chapter VIII—

THE APPLICATION OF THE PRINCIPLE OF THE NEW MAN OUT OF BOTH PARTIES

THE DOCTRINE OF individualism is working havoc in American life. If the individual is an end in himself, then you produce an undisciplined type of character, and consequently an undisciplined country. The desires, the appetites, the passions, the interests of the individual, his position and power, become the driving urge and the goal. And when that happens you are headed for disruption and frustration. That has happened with us. We are an undisciplined people.

If you think that an overstatement look at these three pictures:

1. A high-school boy comes to his principal and in a frustrated way says: "Sir, they tell me that this is a country of individual freedom. But I don't have freedom. I'm told what to do, and I have to do it. I'm told to go to school, and I have to go. I'm told to change to another classroom, and I have to change; to study, and I have to study. Where is my individual freedom?" The youth was serious, for he had taken seriously our doctrine of individual freedom. As a result he was frustrated.

2. A judge, after granting 287 divorces in a four-hour session, said, "If this is a civilization, then we are in a dickens

of a fix." And this was not in Reno, Nevada, where those desiring divorce congregate from all over the country; it was in Augusta, Georgia, at the center of the supposedly conservative South. What was the basic reason for these families' not being able to hold together? Answer: a bald individualism that teaches that the individual's notions, fancies, appetites, egoisms are supreme, and that anything that interferes with them, including marriage vows, should be put aside, for the individual is amenable to nothing beyond himself. The disintegration of the American home is due primarily to a rampant individualism.

3. A doctor came to one of our Ashrams to spend two weeks. He said, "I came here to get something to help my patients. Eighty-five per cent of the patients that come to me are suffering from functional diseases. They are sick in mind and soul and are passing on these sicknesses to their bodies. This last year has seen a phenomenal growth in this type of malady—an almost one hundred per cent growth." Why? The individual, taught that he is an end in himself, suddenly finds an external control laying its hands on him and telling him what to do and what not to do, where to go and where not to go. His life pattern is disrupted, and he is frustrated; so disease sets in.

These three pictures of youth, of married people, and of people in general tell the sickening story of the havoc of rampant individualism. And yet individualism is still blandly taught as though it were the truth, and that in high places in church and state. This last summer I listened to two rare and beautiful souls, with well-trained minds, say before study classes the following: "The individual is of paramount importance," and, "The individual is an end in himself."

Both of those statements are at complete variance with the Christian faith.

The Christian faith does not say: "Seek first the individual—or, in other words, yourself—and everything will be added unto you." It says the very opposite: the individual must lose his life in something beyond himself, and then, and then only, will he find himself. Its clear word is: "Seek ye first the Kingdom of God, . . . and all these things shall be added unto you." Your supreme loyalty and your supreme interest is not to yourself, but to the Kingdom of God. Seek first the kingdom of self, and all these things—happiness, harmony, the very self itself—will be subtracted from you. Is that an impossible idealism or is it stark realism? If we won't listen to the Christian faith, then listen to psychology. "It has been shown that all mistakes, all weaknesses, and all aberrations can be traced back to man's egocentricity," says Dr. Fritz Kunkel. And Alfred Adler, the inventor of the phrase "inferiority complex," says: "All the ills of the human personality can be traced back to one thing, not understanding the meaning of, 'It is more blessed to give than to receive.' " Both the Christian faith and psychology converge upon this point: to find your life, you must lose it in a loyalty to something beyond yourself.

Any system that will not recognize this is at war not only with the Christian faith but also with human nature. This will be startling to many who believe that human nature is constructed on the basis of self-interest and self-interest alone, but it is true nevertheless. For there are three driving urges or instincts in human nature: self, sex, and herd. The self instinct is self-regarding; the herd or social instinct is other-regarding; the sex instinct is partly self-regarding and partly other-regarding. There are then just two great instincts in us: the self-regarding and the other-regarding, the egoistic and the altruistic. If you build life around the self-regarding, you will be at war with yourself because the other-regarding instinct is frustrated. Therefore every self-regarding person, or society, or nation is unhappy and frustrated—at war with itself.

That is the basic trouble with individualism: it is at war with itself, and consequently with others. It is fundamentally unhappy. And yet individualism has a truth in it. The Christian faith recognizes that truth: "Thou shalt love . . thyself." It teaches self-love and rightly so. For if you didn't love yourself, you wouldn't improve yourself. But if the Christian faith had stopped there, it would have fallen into the error of individualism. On the other hand, if it had said, "Thou shalt love thy neighbor," and had stopped there, it would have fallen into the error of collectivism. Collectivism tries to organize life around the other-regarding urge. It too has a truth in it, but only a half-truth. Both individualism and collectivism are half-truths, and life founded on either one of them alone will ultimately go to pieces. Individualism forgets that life is social, and collectivism forgets that life is individual and personal. therefore reject both of them as ways of life. And yet would retain the truth in each. How?

The answer is to be found in the doctrine of the new man out of both parties. The world is in a conflict—a global conflict over two great rival life-patterns, individualism and collectivism. In the kickback from individualism three great movements arose as intended correctives: Fascism Nazism, and Communism. All three of these are intended

126

correctives of individualism, and all three are intended to be organized around the same instinct, and all three are intended to go in the same direction. All three are intended to be organized around the other-regarding instinct and are intended to go in the direction of the enlargement of the area of co-operation. Fascism enlarges the area of co-operation, but stops within the limits of the state with its co-operative endeavor; within the limits of the fascist state there is a co-operative endeavor—a "National Socialism." Nazism enlarges the area of co-operation, but stops within the limits of the race; within the limits of the so-called superior Aryan race there is a co-operative endeavor—a "National Socialism." Communism enlarges the area of co-operation but stops within the limits of the class—the class of the proletariat. They say they are on the way to a classless society, but in the meantime there will be a dictatorship of one class—the proletariat. Within the limits of that class there is a co-operative order—"Socialism." All three of these are going in the direction of the enlargement of the area of co-operation—the application of the herd instinct.

Then if they are all going in the direction of the enlargement of the area of co-operation, why the clashes and wars? The answer obviously is: they all stop short in their co-operative endeavor. If you stop within the limits of the state with your co-operative endeavor, then your attitude toward other states is opposition and antagonism, and other states will combine against you, and there will be clash between states—as now. If you stop within the race with your co-operative endeavor, then other races will combine against you, and there will be clash between races for the supremacy—as now. If you stop within the area of the class with your co-operative endeavor, then other classes will combine against you, and there will be class war—as now.

All three of these stop short and lay the foundation for clash and war. Then what is the remedy? If we cannot go to Fascism, Nazism, or Communism, then where do we go? Back to individualism? We cannot. For individualism is outgrown; it is too small a basis for life. For life is seen to be social as well as individual. Then where do we go? The Christian has the answer in his doctrine of the new man out of both parties. I reject individualism as such, and I reject collectivism as such, and yet I see that each has a truth, and each has an error. Suppose you could get them both to change—that would mean the renunciation of the error in each—and get them both to come to a third position beyond each, gathering up the truth in each, so that out of the two would emerge the new man; would that make peace? It would, for neither one would conquer the other, but something beyond each would conquer both, and yet each would see its truth fulfilled in a higher synthesis; that would lay the foundation for peace—the only peace, the peace of comprehension and fulfillment.

Life as well as thought, according to Hegel, moves through these stages: thesis, antithesis, and synthesis. Thesis gives birth to antithesis, and out of the clash of opposites there emerges the truth in each, comprehended in a higher synthesis. The thesis is individualism; it has given birth to the antithesis, collectivism. Out of the clash of opposites is struggling to be born a synthesis; that synthesis is the Kingdom of God. The Kingdom of God gathers up into itself the truth in individualism and the truth in collectivism and yet goes beyond each. The end is not a compromise, or an amalgam of both, but is a new product—a new man out of both parties.

In the Kingdom of God collectivism is fulfilled, for the Kingdom of God is a divine *society*. It is a social order, and that order is completely totalitarian; it demands the allegiance of everything and everybody in the whole of life. While collectivism is fulfilled in the Kingdom, so also is individualism. For the individual in seeking first the Kingdom of God finds that everything is added to him—including himself. As he loses his life in this ultimate allegiance, he finds it again. It comes back to him, released and free. For he is made for this new order, as the fish is made for the sea, the bird is made for the air; it is his native air, his natural habitat, the homeland of his soul. In obedience to the Kingdom he obeys his deepest self. For the Kingdom of God is within you! It is you—the real you—and when you find it you find yourself. I do not argue; I only testify that when I most belong to the Kingdom I most belong to myself. I am free; I walk the earth a conqueror; the sum total of reality is behind me; I am afraid of nothing. This is life!

But it is not mere impersonal life; it is life that is so intensely personal that you have to spell it Personal. For it is a relationship to an Order, embodied in a Person. It is ultimate, but it is also intimate. Does this personal intimacy with a Person shut me in and make me exclusive? On the contrary it enlarges every fiber of my being, every thought of my mind, every longing of my soul, and universalizes it. I know that this Kingdom cannot, by its very nature, belong to a state, a race, or a class; it belongs to everybody, and to everybody as a person, apart from race, state, or class. For it is truth, and truth by its very nature is universal.

The Kingdom of God is the complete totalitarianism which, when obeyed, gives complete freedom in the total life. Since we wouldn't choose this Kingdom through intelligent choice, the rise of the pseudo-totalitarianisms was inevitable. They rose as a reaction against individualism. God did not inspire their rise, but he has used them as a hammer of judgment upon our selfish individualism. As Dr. Walter Horton says, God has two hands—the hand of grace, and the hand of judgment. If we will not take from the hand of grace, we will have to take from the hand of judgment. We refused to accept the Kingdom of God through the hand of grace, so the hand of judgment fell— the old order is going down in global ruin. Since we wouldn't wash away our selfishness in the blood of Christ, God's Son, we are now having to do it in the blood of our own sons. It is a bitter way—the bitter way of the prodigal who had to come to himself before he would arise and go to his father. Even this bitter catharsis will end only in more bitter disillusionment if, at the end, we do not arise and go to the Father and accept his Kingdom and through it accept our own freedom and fulfillment.

Through this war the worst of the collectivisms—Fascism, Nazism, and Tojoism will probably perish. Then two great powers will be left: America embodying individualism and Russia embodying collectivism. America represents individualism at its best, and Russia represents collectivism at its best. Two great systems will face each other. In mortal combat as to which will master the world? Yes, unless they both decide to change and make a new man out of both parties—a world co-operative man. In that reconciliation on a higher level each will contribute something to the other. For each by itself is incomplete. A combination of individualism and collectivism will give us what we need. We will probably give to Russia the first commandment, "Thou shalt love the Lord thy God," and they will give to us the second, "Thou shalt love thy neighbor as thyself." Both will be richer. For while they represent individualism and collectivism at their best, their best is not good enough. Their answers don't answer. Only God's answer can answer: "It is God's answer that will answer to the Pharaoh." It is only God's answer that can answer to our individual and global need.

And God's answer is Christ! And Christ's answer is himself embodying a Kingdom. He is the new Man through and around whom alone that new man may be produced out of both parties. If that new man cannot be produced, then we are sunk; for the old man is like the demoniac of the Gadarenes, tearing himself to pieces in fratricidal struggle. Christ cured one demoniac until with devils gone he was seated at the Master's feet, clothed and in his right mind. And Christ can do it again—this time on a global scale—and the one seated with contending devils gone, clothed and in his right mind, will be the new man.

The hope of the future is to produce a new man out of both parties—out of individualism and collectivism—that will make peace, the only peace.

Chapter IX—

THE PRINCIPLE OF THE NEW MAN APPLIED TO AMERICAN LIFE

WE HAVE SEEN the possibility of the new man out of both parties applied to the world situation. We must now turn and look at the possibility of this principle applied to American life.

In the preceding chapter I pointed out the possibility that at the end of this conflict will stand two great embodiments —Russia embodying collectivism and America embodying individualism—and that they must both change to come to the new man. What will be the role of the rest of the world in this new man? God may use some of the very smallest nations to help effect this change. Switzerland, content with her mountain home and refusing to enter the race of imperialisms for world territory, became the peace center of the world; she refused to try to grab the world, so the world came to her. And today she is almost the one spared spot of Europe, as if the warring nations were loathe to touch this center of peace. She may again be the instrument of the divine peace—this time decisively, for she may help produce the new man out of both parties. And little Uruguay, experimental ground for social living in Latin America, and Sweden, experimental ground for co-operatives in Europe, may yield themselves to be the instruments of the divine purpose. And India, in jail in this crisis hour, may come out of jail to lead the nations to freedom and peace through the new method of soul force against physical force. China, peace-loving and believing that "all men within the four seas are brothers," may have a decisive part in shaping that new man. And Africa, downtrodden for centuries, may produce a leader who can speak the kindling word about the new man. The two greatest statements spoken in this crisis have been spoken by a Chinese and an African. Madame Chiang Kai-shek said to a great gathering: "There must be no hates, no revenges, only forgiveness and reconstruction." And Haile Selassie said, "We must forgive and reconstruct." These are the soundest moral notes yet uttered, and they were uttered by two people whose nations had suffered terribly. Maybe the white Christian world will be saved by the yellow and the black Christians. Who knows? Palestine, a small, obscure, subject land gave birth to a movement that today in this crisis is the one hope of humanity. God had to pass by Greece with its intellectualism and Rome with its power and take a nation morally responsive to be the instrument of his redemption. It may happen again.

There is Britain. I hope she may slough off empire and be the real Britain—the Britain of democracy. If so, then we can substitute "the Anglo-Saxons" in the places where I use "America."

At any rate I inwardly hope that my own nation may be the instrument through which that new man may arise in world affairs. But if she is, then she herself must be the new man—the new man in miniature. Her message must be her own demonstration. The word of the new man must become flesh. And she has that possibility. For, as I said before, we are the world; the world is in our veins; all nations meet in us; we are the world in epitome. Our demonstration of the new man would be a proving ground for the world. If it can happen here, it can happen anywhere. And it can happen here.

If so, then America, with many divisions running through her life, must come to a new unity. I believe that the Christian faith with its emphasis upon a new man out of both parties can produce that unity. Just as the Christian faith produces the new man out of the conflicts in the individual, in the same way it must produce the new man out of every conflicting situation in every phase of American life. That is its evangelism.

Take the conflict between capital and labor in American industrial life. It is one of the most serious menaces to the life of our land. It is no solution to say, "Hush, hush—we are all Americans," for that does not solve it; it only suppresses it, and a suppressed conflict is the most dangerous. Christians are "the children of light," and therefore believe in bringing up everything and facing it openly and honestly and trying to find a way out. I was once invited with some other ministers to a luncheon arranged by the National Association of Manufacturers. The obvious intention was to convert us as ministers, and through us the Christian Church as far as we had any influence, to the program of the National Association of Manufacturers. It was ably done. They had a philosophy of "free enterprise." They asked me to open the discussion, and I said, "If the purpose of this meeting is to convert us as ministers and through us the Christian Church to the program of this association, I for one hope it won't happen. I do not want to see the Christian Church deliver itself into the hands of your association, nor tie itself to the wheels of industry as such. Just as little do I want the Church to deliver itself into the hands of organized labor as such. But if both capital and labor want a friend—I trust an unselfish friend—to help you both to change and come to a third position beyond the position of each—the new man out of both parties—then I hope the Christian Church will be that unselfish friend of both. For I think that the emergence of that new man will make peace in industry. But if capital tries to conquer labor and suppress it, then there will be no peace; there will be planned revenges, strikes, slowdowns, obstruction. I am also persuaded that if labor tries to conquer capital, again there will be no peace. But if you both change and come to the new man in industry—the co-operative man—that will make peace. For in that new man the legitimate rights of capital and the legitimate rights of labor will be gathered up and embodied. Neither one will conquer the other, but both will be conquered by something beyond themselves—co-operation. The new man will be the co-operative man—co-operating in production, in management, and in the division of profits and losses. Without the sharing of profits and losses the rest would be hollow and meaningless. It must be a thoroughgoing co-operation so that the peace may be thoroughgoing and not merely a patched-up truce. If you want the Christian Church to help produce that new man, then we are at your disposal. But you cannot ask us to play the role of giving the old sick man of selfish interests a periodic shot of kindly advice in the arm so that he may feel a little better—a little more virtuous. We are out to produce the new man."

What I said was rather a bombshell in the purposes of that meeting and caused confusion. But toward the close the leading industrialist of the city arose and said, "I believe the man from India is right. I hope the Christian Church won't give itself either to capital or to labor, but will give itself to getting us both to change; for I think we both need to change, so that we may come to that new man. I think that would make peace in industry." It would.

But the way we are now trying to have peace in industry will not bring peace—is not bringing peace. A personnel man in an industry employing sixty-five thousand men said to me: "I could explode this whole situation by the publication of the facts I have. Management and labor are sullenly facing each other. On both sides unadulterated selfishness reigns. It is blocking everything and interfering with the total efficiency. If we don't have a new attitude on both sides, then there will be an explosion which will rock this country within ten years." This is from a man within industry. Take the statement of Herbert Agar, a newspaper editor now in the armed forces: "Thus class consciousness among U. S. industrialists has made U. S. unions fight a civil war which has been equally degrading to the losing employers and to the victorious unions. Union 'rackets' are largely the result of the type of war that employers waged against the unions." Like has produced like, on both sides. Result? The whole industrial process has slowed down. Even with the cry, "The nation is in danger," ringing in their ears, both sides refuse to bring forth greater effort unless given higher returns in increased profits and wages. The industrial pump is being primed with billions of the nation's wealth, and yet the output is meager comparable to what it might be if there were a new motive. The old motive has worn itself thin. I used to think the American workman was a fast worker. I've changed my mind. There are exceptions of course; but, unless geared to a machine that makes him keep up, he dawdles, doing just as much as is necessary to hold his job and very little more. Why? Is he naturally lazy? No, the least lazy man in the world. But the setup is suffering from dry rot. It lacks motivation. The laborer knows that the more he works the more profits accrue to the owner of capital, and not to him. And, moreover, he knows if he does speed up he will work himself out of a job by overproduction. The clog is in his mind, and that works out into the industrial situation and results in a clogged industrialism.

But change the motivation from competition with his employer to co-operation, then the situation changes. But you cannot change the motivation by saying, "Now let's co-operate." The co-operation can come only when industry is *in fact* a co-operative endeavor. If it is to be, then it must be from top to bottom. Capital and labor must start on the basis of equality—not on the basis of master and servant. That position of master and servant must be renounced. Why should the owner of capital own the business which when labor comes into it becomes a joint enterprise? Before he invests his capital in an industry he owns his capital, but the moment he invests it in the industry the resulting business is due partly to capital and partly to labor. It cannot be run without labor. Then if capital invests the capital, and labor invests brain and brawn and skill, that resultant enterprise is in deed and in truth a co-operative enterprise. By its very nature it is a co-operative enterprise. To twist it so that capital owns and manages and gets the profits and hires and fires a commodity called labor is to prostitute its essential nature. It must go back to what it really is—a co-operative endeavor in which there is co-operation in production, in management, in hiring and firing men, and in the division of profits and losses. Then both labor and capital will come to a new motivation; they will not be working against each other, but for each other. The laborer will know that the more he works the more everybody will get, including himself. The laborers themselves then will co-operate to keep out slackers. It will be to everybody's interest to do so. Moreover capital will have a sense of new motivation. It will lose itself to find itself again. It will lose itself as master and find itself as brother. As master it has incited cupidity, contention, and clash. As brother it will incite good will, co-operation, and a greatly accelerated and efficient industrial order.

A more efficient industrial order is possible. This order periodically jams up at the place of distribution. It has the motive for production, self-interest, but it hasn't the motive for distribution, other-interest. Hence our economy periodically overproduces; then there is unemployment and then depression. These cycles have been recurring with increasing frequency, unless war comes along and eats up the surplus produced. But really there never has been overproduction; there has only been underdistribution. Sumner Welles says: "The problem which will confront us when the postwar period is reached is not primarily one of production. For the world can readily produce what mankind requires. The problem is one of distribution and purchasing power, of providing the mechanism whereby what the world produces may be fairly distributed among the nations of the world, and of providing the means whereby the people of the world may obtain the world's goods and services." And the Archbishop of Canterbury adds: "Industry has been more concerned with the increase of output than with the justice of distribution." Henry Ford, however, says distribution is not the business of industry: "Our business in industry is to produce; . . . distribution is society's part of the work. When it masters distribution as well as industry has mastered production, we shall be sailing ahead again." I think he washes his hands too lightly of the responsibility for distribution, for that would allow industry to operate under self-interest with society supplying the other-interest. That is a false dualism. Industry itself must have operative in itself the two motives of self-interest and other-interest—in other words must be a co-operative order. This will mean a very heavy renunciation on the part of the industrialist: he will renounce being master, with his employees as servants; he will no longer be a boss, but a brother. Will the industrialist lose his life to find it again? If so, then there will be a new birth in our industrial economy—a new efficiency, and a new brotherhood in production.

Moreover it will do something to the soul of both the industrialist and the laborer. Now both are unhappy. Both have to find their happiness outside the industrial machine in off hours—through recreation, diversions, hobbies, causes. Why? For the simple reason that organizing life around self-interest, and self-interest alone, makes both the industrialist and the laborer be at war with themselves. For, as we have noted, the two driving instincts are the self-regarding and the other-regarding. Organizing life around the self-regarding brings the individual into conflict with the other-regarding instinct within him. Hence every self-centered man is in conflict with himself. Give him everything that the self supposedly wants and he will be fundamentally unhappy. He simply cannot be happy, for he is in conflict with the other-regarding urge within him. But put into operation the principle, "Thou shalt love thy neighbor as thyself," and then the self-regarding "Thou shalt love . . . thyself" and the other-regarding "Thou shalt love thy neighbor" will both be fulfilled and will be in operation. The man will be inwardly unified and happy. In that case both the industrialist and the laborer in working for themselves will be working for others, and in working for others they will be working for themselves. It will be a society of mutual aid.

Then the individual in industry will feel that he need not go outside his business to find a sense of vocation; he will find it in his very business. For in working for himself, he will be working for others and will be supplying essential service to the community. His inmost self will be fulfilled. What we need more than almost anything else is the possibility of finding self-fulfillment in our daily work. Then the industrialist and the laborer will go to their daily tasks with a sense of well-being, of comradeship, of partnership in mutual service to each other and to all. That will put oil in place of sand in our industrial life.

It's a far cry from that picture to this one. An industrialist in the steel industry said to me: "Within my business it's the survival of the fittest." And he said it with a wry smile

140

that told of a soul in conflict. Another industrialist at the very center of the industrial life of this nation said: "The only way to treat labor is with lead." And this from a laborer: "I've got to quit hating the boss, and acting like a ———."

America can choose which of those two pictures she desires: industry as mutual slaughter, or as mutual aid; a dog-eat-dog economy, or a brother-help-brother economy. American industrialism can choose one of these three attitudes: (1) "I am my brother's boss," (2) "I am my brother's keeper," or (3) "I am my brother's brother." The first represents autocracy, the second charity, and the third brotherhood. We have outgrown the first; autocracy in Hitler and autocracy in industry are two of a kind, and both must go. Nor will charity do. It is easy to be charitable; it is essential to be just. Only the third, "I am my brother's brother," is essentially right. And only on that basis will an economy be stable.

Will this be realistic? The only realism! For this law of mutual aid is at the basis of life. An industrialist, a student of histology, the science of the structure of animal and plant tissues, said, "I've found a law in the cells; it is the law of mutual aid: each for all and all for each—that is the basis of life in the cells." If that is true, then when we ask that industry be put in line with that law, which is at the basis of life, we are not asking for the impossible. Not to do so is the impossible. For not to do so is to live against life, and you cannot live against life and get away with it. As Marcus Aurelius said: "For we are made for co-operation—like feet, like hands. . . . To act against one another, then, is contrary to nature."

It may be noted that America has seen the necessity of fulfilling the other-regarding urge, so we have organized "service clubs" in American life. These clubs hold within them the cream of our business and professional life. But while these clubs are good they are not good enough, for they put the service motive into an hour and a half a week, when men are off duty, and eating. It is a gesture— a gesture of recognition that the service motive must be put into life. But putting the service motive into an hour and a half a week is pitifully inadequate. The other-regarding motive must be put down at the basis of industry in as fundamental a way as the self-regarding motive now is. In fact they must be equally harnessed as driving urges. "Thou shalt love thy neighbor *as* thyself." When the self-regarding motive and the other-regarding motive are equally basic in our economy, then and then alone will we cease to be at war with God, with one another, and with ourselves. Then our economy will be stable.

Industry needs a philosophy of life behind it—something to lift it to a new level. For it is now a jungle of relationships. The only adequate philosophy of industry I know of is not mine; I discovered it in the Christian faith: "a new man out of both parties." That will make peace, and prosperity, for everybody.

The New Testament speaks of "the resurrection of the just." We would probably have said, "the resurrection of the kind," but the insistence is on the *"just."* There will never be a resurrection of the industrial life of the world unless we decide to be just, and to be basically just means that we will bring capital and labor to a basic equality; then the new man will arise. The New Testament further adds the phrase "the *wisdom* of the just." To be just is not only to be good; it is to be wise. For the phrase could be put this way: "The unwisdom of the unjust." For to hurt your brother is to hurt yourself, and to help your brother is to help yourself. The interests of labor and capital are not two, but one. They go up and down together. To refuse to recognize this is to be just as foolish as the little boy who, when his mother suggested that he pull his feet under the covers, replied, "You don't think I want those cold things in bed with me, do you?" If industry refuses to share with labor the warmth of a co-operative order, then it is its own feet which are out in the cold. To pull the feet of labor under the cover would not only be good; it would be wise.

The only hope for a solution in industry is to get both capital and labor to change and come to a third position, a new man out of both parties. That will make peace.

Chapter X—

FURTHER APPLICATIONS OF THE PRINCIPLE

ALL THROUGH THE National Christian Mission we repeated the plea that there needs to be some constructive force working within American life that will be unity-bringing, that will bridge the gaps in our national life—gaps that are in some cases widening, dangerously so. I am persuaded that the Christian movement is the only force that can bridge those gaps, for by its very outlook and spirit it is fitted and called to do so.

For it has a standing point outside the national life. It descends from the absolute of the Kingdom to all the relativisms that struggle for supremacy. It sees the half-truths in the light of the Truth. Its position is that of detachment, and yet by its insistence upon love as its working force it is thoroughly attached in sympathetic understanding. It is the one movement which is *for* everybody. It is *for* everybody, but against evil which hurts anybody, anywhere. Therefore it is fitted, and the only one that I can see that is fitted, to bridge the gaps in American life.

If the Christian movement is going to bridge gaps, it must begin by bridging the gap between itself and education. The Christian movement and education began life together in America. It was out of the Christian movement that education began and by the Christian movement that education was nurtured. The colonizing powers had little or no interest in the education of the colonists. "When Dr. James Blair . . . went to the attorney-general with a request for a collegiate charter and urged that the people of Virginia had souls to be cared for, he was greeted by the explosion: 'Damn their souls! Let them make tobacco.' " Education was at a very low ebb. In the *Philadelphia Mercury* there appeared in 1735 this notice: "To be disposed of, a likely servant man's time for 4 years who is very well qualified for a clerk or to teach a school, he reads, writes, understands arithmetick, and accompts very well." If education was at such a low ebb that teachers were bought and sold as indentured labor, where did the impulse for education come from? From the Christian movement. Ninety-five percent of the colleges and universities of this country were founded by Christian bodies. Higher education was in the hands of the Church.

Then the state came along and took education out of the hands of the Church, and education was secularized. We do not grumble at this, for the separation of the Church and public education was inevitable. It was too big for the Church to manage. Besides, it was necessary for the Church and education to separate so that each could find its own soul. The Church was so bound up with dogmatism, narrownesses, and the closed mind that it was not fit truly to Christianize education. And education had to separate in order to experiment through the inductive method and gain its own positions, to find its own educational soul.

But now that the separation has taken place it is realized that the separation has left them too separate. This is an increasing conviction on the part of our best educators.

For secularized education with its emphasis upon induction has taught us everything about life except how to live it! It can pick life to pieces, but it doesn't know how to put it together again so that it becomes an integrated whole. It is long on analysis, but short on synthesis. Someone has said that "this age is suffering from the paralysis of analysis." Secular education lacks synthesis; it lacks the power to put life together in great affirmations by which men can live and for which men can die. It has not, and cannot, give youth a cause. As someone has said, "Education has given spokes to the wheel, but no hub." It has given nothing that binds life into central meaning and integration. At the end of a college course the real question is not what you know, but what you love. Unless given a supreme loyalty, life hangs at loose ends. I said to some college students one day, "You have everything. You are a much better generation than mine—more honest, better trained, two inches taller. You have everything except one thing—a cause." A youth arose and said, "But we have a cause." And when I asked him what it was, he replied, "We want to succeed." The tragedy of that was that he not only didn't have a cause; he didn't know what was meant by a cause. He thought success in terms of personal accumulation was a cause. "I want to make my pile"—that was a cause!

Lest the older generation look down on the younger for this moral blindness, let me hasten to say that when I quoted the statement of the student to one of the leading editors of this country his face brightened up and he replied: "Wonderful answer wasn't it?" Where did this younger generation get the idea that success in terms of personal accumulation was a cause? From the older generation. There is nothing wrong with this younger generation except the older! I repeated that one day to a group, and a youngster of twelve years piped up and said, "Say, you said something!" I said only the truth. As I was about to speak to a sorority, the lovely young thing, the president, leaned over at the table and asked, "May I say a word to you before you speak to these girls? They are very careless about religion; they don't go to church. You give them hell; they need it." I did, and they seemed to like it! The next day I spoke to 1,500 bon tons of the older generation at a banquet, and I told them what the girl had said her generation needed. "But," I continued, "I don't think that is the generation that needs it; I think I have it right here before me." And I proceeded to give it to them. I don't think they liked it. For they needed it most!

Why is this older generation unable to give the needed moral guidance to this younger generation? The answer is that the older generation too has been brought up on a secularized education, and except where it has been touched here and there by the Christian faith, outside of education, its mind is secularized and without a cause. Both generations need it. But how can we rectify the blunders of the past and give the rising generation something to live for and die for? Can we put religion back into the educational process? We must, or decay morally as a nation. If our young people get their morals from movies, and their characters from cowboys, or even criminals, then we must expect just what we have—a breakdown in morals.

A movie house complained that they could not run their shows, for the high-school students would rip up the seats with penknives, would turn off the lights and then pour in without tickets in the darkness, and on one occasion actually piled up furniture in a side room and set fire to it. When I read this account to a high-school principal in that city, his reply was: "Well, the movie people had it coming to them. They sowed the wind in their rotten movies, and they are reaping the whirlwind in rotten morals in the youth. There is always a worse outbreak of lawlessness after [a certain popular but morally loose actor] comes on." And yet that principal did not disclaim responsibility by laying the whole blame on the movies; he saw that the place to begin was in the mind and soul of youth, and that the reform had to take place within the educational process itself. It could not be turned over to the churches to accomplish in an hour once a week in Sunday school. I do not minimize what that hour a week does; it is the saving salt of the situation. A teacher said in answer to my inquiry: "Those chosen to be presidents of the student body are invariably fine characters; they are almost invariably young people trained in Sunday schools and young people's organizations." This is good—but not good enough. This leaven of moral and spiritual renewal must go to the rank and file as well as to a few leaders. But how?

Religion and education, having separated, must now be brought together, not occasionally by a lecture, nor merely once a week for weekday religious education—although these are both good—but they must be brought together frankly and openly. Religion must be made a part of the educational process, and teachers must be trained to impart it just as they are trained in any other subject. The fear of sectarian emphasis can be overcome by the fact that now the sectarian emphasis is being transcended in most of our churches and a type of Christianity has been produced that may be imparted without sectarian bias or emphasis. Tens of thousands of such teachers can be found. All it needs is the wholehearted consent of the educational authorities backed by public opinion.

If there is a hesitation on the part of the public officials that such a course would be contrary to our American tradition, let it be recalled that the founders of our nation expressed two views regarding religion and education; one separates them, and the other puts them together. One is in the Bill of Rights added to the Constitution: "Congress shall make no law respecting an establishment of religion, or prohibiting the free exercise thereof." Here they were separated. The other is in the Northwest Ordinance of 1787: "Religion, morality, and knowledge being necessary to good government and the happiness of mankind, schools and the means of education shall be forever encouraged." Here they were brought together. Note: "Religion, morality . . . being necessary . . . , schools . . . shall be forever encouraged." How were religion and morality to be imparted? Through the schools! It is as clear as crystal that while the American tradition demands that there be no established religion, no sectarian favoritism or emphasis, nevertheless it further demands that, "religion, morality, and knowledge being necessary to good government and the happiness of mankind," the inculcation of religion and morality must be through the schools. The idea of a completely secularized education was foreign to the founders of this nation. And it is foreign to the deepest needs of this country. We cannot build a good nation if it is to be a godless nation. There is no character-forming power on earth comparable to real, vital religion.

Perhaps, it may not be amiss to say that I have personally tried the following approach in putting the religious message into public schools. I announce some subject such as "What May a Modern Person Believe?" and then at the close say something like the following: "What do we do about it? Well, if you are a member of the Jewish faith, I would suggest that you go home and talk to your rabbi and say to him, 'I'm committed. I see what I must do: I'm going to give myself to God and the Temple.' If you have a Roman Catholic heritage, go home and say to your priest, 'I'm committed. I'm going to give myself to God and to the Church.' And if you have an Evangelical or Protestant heritage, go home and say to your pastor: 'I'm committed. I'm going to give myself to God and to the Church.' " And then I tell them what they may write in the flyleaf of their Bibles as their decision. I have done that in scores of high schools and colleges across this country, and never once have I had an unfavorable reaction. The public-school teacher could teach the Christian faith with its Jewish heritage and background, and then go on and say: "I have taught you these basic principles and ideas; now go home, and if you feel disposed, identify yourself with the church of your choice—Jewish, Catholic, or Evangelical."

Would the students themselves respond? My reply would be that if I had one place and only one place, to invest my life in America I would unhesitatingly choose the high school. The high-school students are the finest group of young people we've ever had—eager, responsive, and wanting something to live by and live for. But they must not be talked down to, or merely told funny stories to catch them. They want a philosophy of life and more—they want power to live by. And they are bright! They are facing questions in the high school that we faced in the college in my day. The place of life decision is in the high school. But one who knew high schools better than perhaps anyone else in America disagreed with me over that statement and said, "The age of life decision and of gaining life direction has now been pushed back into the junior high." An able worker among youth agrees with her. In any case, don't talk down to the high-school student. I repeat: he is intelligent. A youth of fifteen said to his mother: "Mother, I don't think some of the older people got what Stanley Jones was talking about tonight. I sat between two women, and their faces were blank—and, Mother, one of them yawned!" Another student of about the same age said to me: "I didn't think you would make the grade tonight. You made it last night, but I didn't think you would make it tonight. But I believe you did." Another: "Say, the thing I liked was the way you put it up, the way you marshaled your facts." I was wondering whether he was getting it, and he was wondering how I was putting it up!

But once a high-school assembly came near getting me— at the very jump-off. I was about to speak to about 3,500 rollicking, roaring high-school students all pepped up for a crucial football game. The principal had suggested in introducing me that this day was the seventy-fifth anniversary of the extending of the telegraph through Omaha. When I arose to speak I remarked that it was one thing to have these inventions and it was another thing to decide what you're going to do with them; it is one thing to have the telegraph, but what do you telegraph? Then I remarked that when the transcontinental telephone was put through from coast to coast in South America the first message that went across was, "Have you any beer?" At that the students set up an uproar of applause, as much as to say, "Wouldn't we like to have some!" They were pulling my leg! I knew I'd have to get them in the first moments, or I would lose them. One Episcopal bishop was howled down in a high school—no respect for the cloth! So I paused and said, "I'm puzzled about that applause. It may mean that you were applauding the imbecility of that question, 'Have you any beer?' If not, then you were applauding your own imbecility." They gasped, applauded, and then I knew I had them, and could say anything to them. When I showed I wasn't afraid of them and hit them between the eyes—good-naturedly—they were ready to listen to anything I had to say. At heart they were inwardly sound.

I was about to speak to three thousand students in the gym of a state college on "Sadie Hawkins Day," a day when the students came to the assembly in outlandish rube costumes. As the assembly was the first time they had seen each other in these costumes, the place was one seething mass of roaring, rollicking young humanity. I was to speak to *that!* And I was to speak on, "What May a Modern Person Believe?" It seemed impossible. The dean frankly said so. But in two minutes those students were as silent as death and gave a pin-drop silence as I spoke to them for three quarters of an hour. At the close I had to get up and bow to them to get them to stop applauding—and that on a purely Christian appeal, and on Sadie Hawkins Day!

No matter what the exterior may be, outlandish costumes

152

or what not—and by the way, I told them in the beginning that they did not really need to dress up especially to be outlandish; all they had to do was wear their regular clothes! —nevertheless the heart of this younger generation is really sound. And I love them. Sometimes in spite of! I was talking to an outdoor meeting, and on the front row was a girl, dressed in pants and a shirt, sprawled on her back with her hands behind her head, looking up at me. I had to talk over *that!* I inwardly wished she'd sit up. But I found she did; every time something struck her she sat up and wrote down a note in a notebook. "Oh," I said to myself, "this younger generation may sprawl in indecorous attitudes and outlandish costumes, but if you say something they will sit up and take notice, and even take notes; so you'd better say something, for they're really listening, and they're wanting something." They are! With all their faults they are the best generation of youth we've ever had. And they take to reality like a trout takes to a fly.

To deprive such a generation of moral and spiritual guidance is a crime against them and the future. Religion and education must come together to accomplish the most important task in American life: the task of giving youth a faith to live by and a cause to live for. A prominent educator has said: "Education for a hundred years has been busy at the task of freeing itself from religion, and it will probably spend the next hundred years freeing itself from the state." It can free itself from the state only if it gives itself to a loyalty higher than the state—the Kingdom of God.

But let us make it clear: we have no desire to dominate education by dogmatism. Education was right in shaking itself free from that domination. But now that both religion and education are free, they are free to enter a new co-operation, on a new basis, on a higher level; a new man can emerge out of both parties. What we desire is not domination but permeation—the permeation of the whole educational process with a new spirit, directing it toward great goals and giving youth a cause.

Religion and education must come together and form a new man out of both parties. That will make peace, and it will also make a new America.

Chapter XI—

THE NEW MAN OUT OF SCIENCE AND RELIGION

IN OUR LAST chapter we urged the necessity of bringing together the Christian movement and the educational movement. No deeper necessity exists in American life. To this most people would agree. But this lingering doubt is in many minds: Aren't the two approaches to life so different that their coming together will be difficult, if not impossible? Isn't education committed to the scientific method—the method of induction, working out from the facts to conclusions? And isn't religion committed to the method of deduction—the method that starts from a proposition and works down to life, hunting for evidence to prove that proposition? One works up from the facts, and the other works down from a starting point—an absolute. Aren't these hopelessly opposed by their very nature?

Even some leading religious thinkers think so. Dr. Shelton Smith in his book *Faith and Nurture* ends his able discussion with these words: "What kind of religion shall the public school teach—the religion of the churches or the religion of humanistic experimentalism? Sooner or later this must become the focal point of a crucial battle. On its outcome largely hangs the fate of democratic culture in America." (P. 202.)

In a discussion which took place some time ago in *The Christian Century* between the editor, Dr. C. C. Morrison, and Professor Hornell Hart the conclusion seemed to be about the same. The end of the discussion seemed to be this: "You haven't seen this Man," said one, and, "You haven't seen this method," said the other. One worked from Christ, the Man, down; and the other worked from the method up. One was the method of Christianity working from revelation down to life; the other was the method of science working from the facts out to conclusions. But they never seemed to meet. The end was inconclusive, and the discussion left you with a sense of frustration and incompleteness. But religion and science can and must meet. But how?

The thing that seemed missing in the above discussion was the recognition that the God who revealed himself through Jesus Christ—perfectly and finally, as I believe—is the same God who created the universe and who built into that universe the laws of the Kingdom of God. It is true that the Kingdom of God comes as men individually and corporately accept it. But it is also true that the Kingdom of God *is*. It is built into the nature of reality, is the way that reality works. When you discover those laws underlying reality you discover the laws of the Kingdom. For this is "the Kingdom prepared . . . from the foundation of the world"—built into the structure of reality as the very laws of its being. Jesus said: "The Kingdom of God is within you." It is written into your tissues, your nerve cells, your blood, into you. Another version (Twentieth Century) puts it: "The Kingdom of God is already among you." It is written into your relationships with each other; it is the way you are made to live corporately; it is the law of our corporate life. Individually and collectively when we live according to the laws of the Kingdom, we live; when we don't, we perish.

But these laws of the Kingdom are written not merely into the human being and his relationships; they are written into the constitution of nature. The New Testament says: "Without him [Christ] was not anything made that was made" (John 1:3); "By whom [Christ] also he made the worlds" (Heb. 1:2); "All things were created by him [Christ], and for him: . . . and by him all things consist," or hold together (Col. 1:16-17). These passages by three different writers make it plain that the touch of Christ is upon all creation, that creation is made to work in the Christian way; for "all things were created by him, and for him"—they are made *for* him, made to work in his way and in no other way. I cannot admit that this is true of human life and relationships but it is not true of the physical universe. The physical universe is also made to work in the Christian way. Treat the physical universe in an unchristian way and it will go back on you. Treat it in a Christian way and it will respond to you.

True, you say; but what about the law of the survival of the fittest in lower nature? Is it not ruthless and unchristian? It may be sub-Christian, but it is not anti-Christian. For it is right that in a purely physical environment the physically fit should survive and pass on their qualities to the next generation. For suppose the unfit survived and passed on their qualities? That would mean deterioration and ultimate extinction. It would be no kindness to allow the unfit to survive and propagate their kind, for that would provide for the extinction of the species. In a purely physical environment this law of the survival of the fittest is right and beneficent. When you come to man, the law of survival is the same: the morally and spiritually fit survive, and the morally and spiritually unfit perish—perish for they are out of harmony with reality.

If there are Ten Commandments in the Bible, there are ten laws written into the constitution of reality. They are these:

1. The universe is a universe of moral consequence; you reap what you sow.

2. The morally and spiritually fit survive; the rest perish.

3. The Christian way is written into the structure of the universe.

4. Humility and obedience are the secret of knowledge and power.

5. An organism can expend as much as it receives and no more; therefore receptivity is the first law of life.

6. The second law of life is: you must lose your life to find it again—self-realization comes through self-renunciation for a cause.

7. Greatness comes through service and only through service.

8. Love is the fundamental law of human relationships.

9. Life is an eternal growth; when you cease to grow you begin to cease to live, you begin to die.

10. All life is lifted by self-sacrifice—by a cross.

If these ten laws are written into the constitution of things and not merely in a sacred book, then it would seem that the Christian way is the natural way to live: it is the way written into nature, and it is the way written in the revelation in Christ. Butler in his *Analogy* got this far in his thinking:

"He who believes that the author of Revelation and the author of Nature are one and the same must expect the same difficulties to be found in Revelation as are to be found in the constitution of Nature." He got as far as parallelisms in difficulties. We have come a long way since then. We see parallelisms in likenesses. Jesus saw them. He kept saying, "The Kingdom of God is like unto" some fact in nature. He lifted up the laws underlying the universe, and they were the very laws of the Kingdom.

We therefore cannot accept the dualism that there are two Gods—one of grace and another of nature. There is one God, and he is the author of both. Christ revealed in his own person and life the laws underlying the universe. What is covert in the universe became overt in him. He is the revelation of God, and of the universe that God created. Reality is shot through and through with Christ. He is woven into the very texture of its being, the soul of its soul.

If that is true, then it has important implications: go far enough with the facts, wherever you find them, and they will bring you out at the place of Christ. That is my profoundest conviction. If I did not believe that, I could not be a Christian with the consent of all my being. But does life verify it? I believe that the discovery of the facts, when they are facts and not half-truths, is leading in one direction and in only one direction—in the direction of Christ. Let the scientist, therefore, begin with the facts, and let him go far enough with those facts, and he will come out at the fact of Christ. He may not get to Christ; he may stop short; but at least his facts will be pointing in the direction of Christ as their fulfillment.

Let men begin anywhere they will and honestly follow the facts and see what happens. Take an unlikely place to find Christ—in our competitive commercial world, a jungle. And yet the vice-president of a leading bank in Chicago says: "The outstanding necessity of banking is unselfishness." Another banker puts it this way: "We have found out that it doesn't pay to break a creditor. If he goes down, the situation goes down with him. It is better to help him to his feet, for if you save him, you save a situation as well. And that's better for the bank." How did they arrive at the fact that unselfishness is the way the universe backs? The facts took them by the hand and brought them out at that place. Take another place. A management engineer says: "The great engineering word is awareness of people." The engineering word! But that is the Christian word! The very essence of the Christian word is to be aware of people—to love them as you love yourself. When Daniel Willard, head of the Baltimore and Ohio Railroad, was asked what the outstanding qualification for a successful executive is he replied: "The ability and the willingness to put yourself in the other person's place." But that is Christian! When Professor William H. Kilpatrick says, "The greatest discovery of modern education is: He that saveth his life shall lose it, and he that loseth it for a cause shall find it again," he simply states after patient research what Jesus stated straight out of the heart of reality.

When these men working laboriously and painstakingly through the facts come out at a Christian position, do I say, "Oh no, you should have started with Christ?" Not at all. I say to them: "My brother, give me your hand. We are coming out at the same place. I began with Christ and worked down to your facts; I see them in the Master Light of all my seeing. I stumbled on him as I blindly groped in desperate moral need. You lifted your eyes from the facts as you patiently sifted them and found they are pointing in a certain direction—the direction of Christ. We are not rivals; we are brothers! I hope you will go far enough and not only discover the fact of Christ but surrender to him, and then and then only you will know the full meaning of him. Surrender to him—would that be foreign to your method? As I understand it, it fits in. For unless you surrender to the facts as a little child, unless you give up all preconceived notions and are willing to follow wherever nature will lead you, you will know nothing. That is your method, isn't it? It's mine too! So in goal and in the method of getting to that goal we are not far apart. In fact we are together. You are the merchantman seeking the pearl of great price, weighing here and rejecting there, until you come across *the* pearl; then you go off and sell all you have to buy that pearl. I am the wayfarer who stumbled across a treasure hid in a field—almost accidentally stubbed my toe against it—and went off and sold all I had to buy that field. Your way is long and laborious; mine is intuitive and swift, but it is the same way. We are one—companions of the Way!"

Suppose, then, religion would give up its dogmatic close-mindedness and, while retaining its stand at the place of Christ, submit the whole thing to the verdict of the facts—to the verdict of life? And suppose science would give up its dogmatic close-mindedness too and, while retaining its method of induction, submit the whole thing to the verdict of the facts—to the verdict of life? What would happen? They wouldn't be six inches apart. In fact they would not be that far apart—they would be one. Each would contribute something to the other, and out of the two would arise a new man. That would make peace.

Someone asked me how I would typify Christian education, and I replied: "I would have a statue of a youth entering college, uncertain, uncouth, but eager. The first door he faces would lead to a room where all ways of life are studied. The next room would be a room where the Christian faith is studied; for I take it that, after studying the various ways, he would find that the universe backs the Christian way. Then there would be a third room, a little chapel where he would dedicate himself to this way. Then outside beyond these three rooms I would have another statue of the same youth, now emerging from his college course—facing away from the institution toward the rising sun, his face assured and confident, for two figures are beside him, Religion and Science, each with a hand upon his shoulder, and both pointing in the same direction toward the rising sun. And thus under the guidance of religion and science—two approaches to life—each corroborating the other, he goes forth to meet the day."

The coming together of religion and science would produce a new man out of both parties; that would make peace, and it would make a new age.

Chapter XII—

BRIDGING THE GAPS

ONE OF THE places where American life must be bridged is at the gap between the scientific movement for health and the Christian movement for health. These two movements, have gone in different directions. The reason for this is easy to discover. When the main stream of Christian faith accepted a dualism in life and began to confine itself largely to the "spiritual," then physical health was relegated to the cults. This was to the credit of the cults and to the discredit of the orthodox. For healing has been in the Christian movement from the beginning; it was in the person of its Founder. Jesus cured disease as an integral part of the coming of the Kingdom; it was the Kingdom active within the body. He himself was never ill, that we know of, and he radiated health and healing. Merely to touch him was to be well. His immediate disciples took up the same emphasis. The Christian movement meant health for the total life. Life was a unit.

In the rediscovery of this original note the cults went too far. Some of them said, "All disease is mental. Cure the mind, and so-called physical disease will drop off as a dead leaf." Others said, "No doctor but God." These two attitudes estranged the scientific movement for health, for the medical men knew that disease was not merely in the mind; it could be in the tissues, and it was very real. They knew also that where scientific medicine is in operation the average length of life has gone up from twenty-one years in the sixteenth century to sixty-two years in this century. At the same time they began to see more clearly that the contention of some of the cults had a truth in it: one could pass on the sicknesses of the mind and the soul to the body. The American Medical Association has said officially that about fifty per cent of all diseases are rooted in the mental and spiritual and fifty per cent in the physical. Some individual doctors estimate as high as eighty-five per cent of diseases are rooted in the mental and spiritual and only fifteen per cent in the physical.

If this is the actual situation, then obviously the medical profession, out of sheer necessity, must turn to the Christian faith, which specializes in mental and spiritual healing, to help them in their task of making the whole person well. Many medical people, turning to psychiatry for help, find it often helpful but inadequate, especially if the psychiatrist is pagan. In that case he can pick people to pieces, but he cannot put them together again on any higher level through great affirmations about life and destiny. This emphasis on analysis and lack of emphasis on synthesis leaves many of the analyzed more disrupted than ever. Self-knowledge is not enough. That knowledge must be followed by a power that can lift people out of themselves and give them faith and courage and a loyalty to Someone beyond themselves. That and that alone will free them from themselves.

A working alliance between the scientific and the Christian movements for health is necessary and inevitable. Can each wholeheartedly accept that alliance? Certainly the Christian can, for this connection between mental and spiritual states and physical diseases is already a part of his faith. Let us look at a few passages which bring this connection clearly to light. "A mind at ease is life and health, but passion makes man rot away." (Prov. 14:30—Moffatt.) "A glad heart helps and heals: a broken spirit saps vitality." (Prov. 17:22—Moffatt.) "My health is wasting under my woe, my life eaten away with sorrow, . . . my body falls to pieces." (Ps. 31:9-10—Moffatt.) "So long as I refused to own my guilt . . . life ebbed away; . . . my body dried up, as in summer heat." (Ps. 32:3-4—Moffatt.) "Banish all worries from your mind, and keep your body free from pain." (Eccles. 11:10—Moffatt.) "Some, weakened by their sinful ways, were sick and suffering through evil-doing; they had a loathing for all food, were on the verge of death." (Ps. 107:17-18—Moffatt.) Jesus connected wrong attitudes and physical disease: "Later on Jesus met him in the temple, and said to him, 'See, you are well and strong; commit no more sins, lest something worse befalls you.'" (John 5:14—Moffatt.) Yet he did not connect all disease with sin: "And his disciples asked him, 'Rabbi, for whose sin—for his own or for his parents'—was he born blind?' Jesus replied, 'Neither for his own sin nor for his parents'.'" (John 9:2-3—Moffatt.) Paul states that "the body is . . . meant . . . for the Lord." (I Cor. 6:13—Moffatt.) That is, it is meant to work in a Christian way; it comes to its own only as it is under the direction of the spirit of Christ.

Can the scientific movement wholeheartedly accept the fact that the mental and spiritual is often the decisive factor in the curing of disease and in maintaining health? Dr. Irving Cutter answers in these words: "We must recall that the intestinal tract can mirror with fidelity every emotional state. Unless the disturbance is relieved, it may settle down to chronic disorder." Dr. Walter C. Alvarez, stomach specialist of the Mayo Clinic, says that seventy-five per cent of stomach disorders are not structural but functional—there is nothing wrong with the stomach; it has been upset by wrong emotional states.

In the Battle Creek Sanitarium this experiment was carried on. A dog with a happy disposition worked his way into everyone's affections at the sanitarium. He was irresistible. The doctors operated on him and found that the marrow in his bones was a beautiful pink—it was filled with red corpuscles. The wound healed almost immediately. Then word was passed down the line that the dog was to be treated with indifference. No one was to pay any attention to him. Some repulsed his advances with gruffness. The dog pined away under this changed treatment. He would stay under tables and sofas. His spirits drooped. Again he was operated on. The marrow in his bones was found to be a dull brown, almost bereft of red corpuscles. The wound healed very slowly, and infection was feared. Then the treatment changed. Everybody was instructed to be friendly again. The dog responded very slowly to this renewed friendship. He had been let down once, so he was suspicious. But he finally responded, and his spirits returned. His tail began wagging; he was his joyous self again. Once more he was operated on, and this time his marrow was again a healthy pink and full of red corpuscles. Again the wound healed quickly. It was obvious that the emotional states of the dog changed the very marrow in his bones. This illustrates what can happen to the health of a human being when subjected to wrong treatment by society, or thrown off balance by his own wrong reactions to life.

If the states of mind and soul can penetrate in their effects clear through to the marrow of the bone, then it is obvious that to treat only the physical and disregard the mental and spiritual is to be unscientific. Such treatment disregards a large proportion of the facts, and to disregard facts is to be unscientific. The scientific movement for health, to remain scientific, must deal with the mental and spiritual. But how can it, unless it enters an alliance with the Christian faith? I say "the Christian faith," for the modern man is shut up to the Christian faith or no faith. There is no living alternative. It is that or nothing. In that alliance the medical man must either get a living faith for himself which transforms him and makes him rhythmical and harmonious and life-imparting, or he must ally himself with those in the Christian faith who have the root of the matter in themselves and can impart it—preferably the ministers. The Christian way cannot be imparted outside oneself. You cannot be a problem dealing with problems. The whole thing must be reality.

On the other hand, if there is to be a working alliance between these two movements, then the ministers of religion must prepare themselves mentally and spiritually for this alliance. They must know something of the background of psychology and be willing to work with doctors in a scientific as well as a religious way. A willingness to work wholeheartedly with the doctors often disposes the patient to heed the Christian side. A lady wrote me this week that when I said to her, "I would take the doctor's verdict," something was released in her and her arthritis was relieved

—she thinks cured. She had perhaps unconsciously resented my statement that arthritis is often caused by wrong mental and spiritual states, such as worry, fear, anxiety. She told me she didn't think hers was rooted in any wrong emotional attitude. My reply was, "Perhaps not. I would take the doctor's verdict." When she saw that I was prepared to accept the physical basis for the arthritis she let down her barriers, faced the facts, found that in truth the arthritis was the result of emotional tensions, surrendered those tensions, and was well. When she returned home the doctor remarked, "You look ten years younger. What's happened?" She told him! He probably responded inwardly, if not outwardly, "In view of what's happened to you, I would take the minister's verdict!" There was a working alliance.

I have been insisting that there should be a demonstration center set up in America where the best in surgery, the best in medicine, the best in psychiatry, and the best in Christianity could be brought together and, working as a team, treat the whole person and make out of him a healthy, adjusted, harmonious, adequate person. Twenty-five leading surgeons, medical men, psychiatrists, and clergymen after a whole day's discussion agreed that such an institution could and should be set up. Such a venture was the next step. The place was selected for demonstration, but the war has blocked the plans. If such a place could be set up with the right personnel and spirit, it might begin a new era in public health.

If the scientific movement and the Christian movement could be brought together on a higher level, then out of the two would arise a new man. And then instead of misunderstanding, non-co-operation, or mere tolerance there would be peace—the peace of a living co-operation.

There is another deep cleavage in American life which needs to be closed up and healed. It is the cleavage between races, especially between the white and the colored races. The tension is growing. In some ways this is discouraging, but in some ways it is hopeful. It is hopeful in that the tensions themselves have arisen out of the fact that the colored races have awakened from their apparent apathy and acceptance of the unjust *status quo* and have now begun to demand on a large scale equality of opportunity in American life. The diehards will resist this demand, often in the name of superior paternalism. Said a white woman from Tuskegee, Alabama, "We love the Negro, *as a Negro*"—meaning "as subservient." She was probably unknown outside of her immediate circle and probably contributed little to the welfare of the human race. But she came from a town where lived a man known throughout the civilized world, who contributed more to the agriculture of the South than any other man who ever lived. Yet she would have Dr. George Carver subservient! By the three great tests of worth-whileness—character, ability, and achievement—she should have been subservient to him! But I do not want anyone to be subservient. I want equality of opportunity to everybody.

Nor am I hopeless that a solution will be found. I can see hope for the solution of race coming through seven streams of influence.

1. *Race prejudice is not inherent; it is socially imposed.* The child knows nothing of it. The children of missionaries,

born in a land of color, know nothing of race prejudice until they see it in the attitudes of society. If race prejudice is socially taught, then its opposite, race appreciation, can be taught. A campaign of education in race appreciation put through our public school system could in large measure wipe out race prejudice in one generation. For instance, a junior high school with a colored minority elected a Negro boy president of the student body. A senior high shcool elected a Japanese boy president of the student body. In each case they chose the boy outstanding in character and achievement. They had no prejudice, for they had been taught none.

2. *The nature of the universe guarantees that no solution not based on right will ever be stable.* The moral universe will upset situations until they come to a basis of complete justice and equality. The instability of race relations around the world arises out of the fact that they are not on a just and equal basis. If men are not prepared to bring those relations to a just and equal basis, then they must be prepared to live in perpetual turmoil and strife. The nature of the moral universe will guarantee that instability. The upset relationships do not come from "agitators," as the diehards suppose. The real agitators are the unconquerable instincts of mankind which will not accept slavery and injustice. And the moral universe agrees with them and upsets any unjust and unequal situation.

3. *The third line of solution is the Christian faith.* Its teachings in regard to race are as clear as crystal. "There is no room for Greek and Jew [race distinction], circumcised and uncircumcised [religious cult distinction], barbarian, Scythian [cultural distinctions], slave, or free man [social

and economic distinction]; Christ is everything and everywhere." (Col. 3:11—Moffatt.) In a parallel passage (Gal. 3: 28—Moffatt), "There is no room for male and female"— sex distinction—is added. In the Christian conception a man is a man—a man "for whom Christ died." When Peter was called to go to the house of a man of another race, he hesitated—his racial past was inhibiting him—but he said, "The Spirit bade me go with them, making no distinction." (Acts 11:12—A.R.V.)

This, then, is clear: if we have room for race prejudice, we have no room for Christ, for in him "there is no room" for race prejudice. If we make distinctions, then we break with the Holy Spirit, who tells us as he told Peter, "Go, . . . making no distinction." Another spirit is substituted for the Holy Spirit—the unholy spirit of race prejudice. We are not different from others.

The world expects the Christian Church to be different, and despises it when it isn't. An interracial luncheon was arranged by the federation of churches at the best hotel in a borderline city. The hotel authorities thought that since the price of the luncheon was $1.25 not many Negroes would come. Of the five hundred tickets sold two hundred were bought by Negroes. The hotel management got cold feet and wanted to call off the luncheon. The secretary of the federation replied, "We won't threaten you, but if you do call it off we will have to tell the churches why." "Give us till three o'clock to decide," the management replied. At this meeting they proposed that the Negroes go up to the luncheon by the service elevator at the back. "No," replied the secretary, "we cannot do that. We are a church federation." "Then," asked the manager, "could both groups go up by the service elevator?" The mayor and the heads of various service and civic and women's clubs were to be present; would they relish going up by a service elevator at the back? It might do them good to see how other people have to go up! It was decided to do that rather than call off the luncheon. But the bellboys apparently were instructed, for they called out as the guests began to arrive, "This way to the church federation luncheon"—and this in a loud voice. The apparent meaning was that they were saying to the other guests in the lobby, "This is a church affair. They do these things; it's not the hotel." It was revealing. "They expect us to be different," I said to myself. "Then we ought to be different. And by the grace of God we will be!" The world has given us the cue: *Be different!*

Therefore I believe, and have advocated for a number of years, that every white church should take in at least one colored member as an equal and respected member of that church, and every colored church should take in at least one white person on the same basis. This would not be a solution, but it would be a symbol—a notice to the outside world that we have our own principles and intend to put them in operation in areas over which we have control.

I was scheduled to speak to an interracial mass meeting in a large city in the deep South. The mayor had heard what I had said about the death of democracy in another city and wanted to call off the meeting. When I was consulted over the long-distance telephone I could reply that I was not intending to speak on the race question but on another subject. Had I intended to speak on the race question, I should have had to stick to it, even if the meeting were called off. This information about the subject relieved the tension, and the proposed meeting went forward. There were 1,500 Negroes and about 2,500 whites present. I began with this preface: "I see I am to speak to an interracial group, but I shall not address you as races, but as persons. I'm a Christian, and a Christian is one who looks on a man as a man, apart from race and birth and color. To him a man is no longer a man; he is a man 'for whom Christ died.' So I shall address you as persons." I then went on and gave my address. As we drove away, a Negro bishop and pastor were in the car with me. They burst out with this: "No, you didn't say anything on the race question! You said everything there is to be said in your preface. If that is the Christian position, then you need say no more. For that says everything."

The Christian faith is clearly on the side of a solution.

4. *The fourth line of solution is the findings of modern science.* Those findings are growingly conclusive: there are no permanently inferior or superior races; there are only undeveloped and developed races. There is a basic humanity, modified here and there by culture. There are no biological differences between man and man, only cultural differences. Given the same stimulus and incentive, human nature around the world will come out about the same. The I.Q.'s of white and colored children in New York City came out about the same. I've asked principals of high schools where white and colored children attend if there is any difference between the examination results of the two races, and every single one has said that there is no difference. There might be a slight modification as the result of cultural heredity, but otherwise none. Twenty-two Negro students went up for government aviation examination in

competition with students from many of the great universities of the country, and the Negro students stood out at the top with a general average of 94.2 per cent. There are fewer washouts proportionally among Negro candidates for aviation than among white candidates. Frank Lambert, a white instructor of aviation at Tuskegee, says, "National or racial characteristics have little or no bearing on skills and abilities and aptitudes." The historian A. J. Toynbee says, "The so-called racial explanation of differences in human performance and achievement is either an ineptitude or a fraud." Carey McWilliams in his able book *Brothers Under the Skin* says, "In the face of this mounting wealth of scientific evidence, it is simply no longer tenable to pretend that 'backward races' cannot acquire the fundamentals of civilized life." Dr. Ruth Benedict says, "We must accept all the implications of our human inheritance, one of the most important of which is the small scope of biologically transmitted behavior and the enormous role of the cultural process in the transmission of tradition. . . . Not one item of man's social organization, of his language, of his local religion, is carried in the germ cell." The National Industrial Conference Board issued a report in 1941 saying that with respect to ability and skill, regularity of attendance, and many other tests, Negroes compare very favorably with the whites. *Modern Industry* in its issue of May, 1942, reported that "out on the production lines Negroes are proving that there is no color line in skill and efficiency."

Science, both theoretical and practical, is corroborating what the Christian faith has always taught: the soul, brain, and body of humanity is basically one, modified here and there by culture. Those who try to perpetuate the idea of inherent superiorities and inferiorities are outdated and out-grown; both knowledge and life have gone beyond them. Both science and religion can say with a sociologist, "Race prejudice is a social, not a racial—that is, not a biological— phenomenon."

5. *The fifth line of solution is that of democracy.* Democracy is founded on the belief in, and the possibilities of, a man as a man. "America's constitution, like Christianity," argues *Fortune*, "is based on the principle that every man is born with the inalienable right to equality of opportunity. Whether or not this assumption is 'realistic,' we must stick to it, or change sides." If we are true to the principles of democracy, we must make an economy in which everybody, regardless of race, color, creed, or sex, can repeat the pledge of allegiance to the flag: "one Nation, indivisible, with liberty and justice for all"—and we must mean the *"all."*

6. *The sixth line of solution is the character and achievements of other races.* The white race, starting as barbarians for the most part, has been subjected to the stimulus and inspiration of the Christian faith for two thousand years. Their superiority has been a superior stimulus. The colored races, for the most part, have had that stimulus and inspiration for a few generations only. Give them the impact of a character-making and a stimulating faith over a few more generations and the differences of character and achievement will fade out. A group of Southern white men asked me for a letter of introduction to Dr. George Washington Carver in order that they might interview him. He was so busy achieving results in science for both white and colored that he didn't have time to stop for casual interviews. It's a long cry from the Negro slave standing in awe

of the "master of the big house" to the descendants of the "master of the big house" asking for an introduction to a former slave—and asking for it because of what he was and what he had done. But that span of eighty years marks the most amazing progress of any group, of any race, in a similar length of time.

The Negro is not a problem; he is a possibility, one of the greatest possibilities in American life. The problem is in us as white people—in our prejudices, in our folly of not gladly and ungrudgingly accepting with gratitude the contribution the Negro could make to our personal and collective lives. "Not to take that contribution," said the white principal of Hampton Institute, "is like refusing to accept a personal gift of a million dollars." It is—and worse! Seventy-five per cent of the colored waiters in the restaurant at the Pennsylvania Railway Station in New York are college graduates. When I asked one of them why they were waiters he replied, "No other lines of employment are open to us." It is national stupidity and inefficiency not to utilize the brains and training of these citizens. I found one graduate in chemistry of a great state university working as a cook in a private home, cooking for two people—all his training and ability unutilized. "I sought for two years for a job as a chemist, but nothing opened, so I was compelled to take this," he said. These two people were graciousness itself to him, but their attitude could not atone for the central wrong done to him by a prejudiced society. Prejudice is culturally, economically, and nationally expensive. It should be ended.

But how? The Christian is the one person who has the answer. He sees, by the very preconceptions of his faith, the whole matter in a world setting, on a global basis. He sees that there will be an inevitable clash between that one-third white minority and the two-thirds colored majority unless we can head it off. How can we head it off? By one group dominating the other? That will never make peace. It will lay the foundations for planned revolt and war. There will be nothing but struggle down through the exhausting centuries. The only possible way to make peace is to create a new man out of both parties—a co-operative man.

Each has something to give to the other. There are qualities in the inheritance of each that would be mutually helpful. The black and white keys of a piano have often been referred to as representing the relationship—neither set of keys competing, but the two working together to produce harmony, a greater harmony than either alone could achieve. Or, to change the figure, God is an artist. He has made many colors, each setting off the other. Someone had a tulip bed with many colors, but something was missing. He inserted a black tulip, and this black tulip set off the colors of the rest. We lack the artistry of God when we think in terms of one exclusive color.

There is the fear that if we take the attitude of appreciation instead of exclusiveness there will be intermarriage. This need not be, for usually people will find their mates within their own social group. The white New Zealander and the colored Maori live together side by side on the basis of social and economic equality, each proud of the other, but with almost no intermarriage. It could be the same with us. Suppose a few rare marriages did occur, would that not be better than the blood intermingling that is now clandestinely taking place on a very low level? The fear of blood mixture is a bugaboo, for we are all mixed. There is no such thing as a pure race. Ellsworth Huntington in his *The Character of Races* says that the European, and consequently the American, is made up of three strains: the Caucasian, the Mediterranean, and the Negroid. The cold winters have bleached out the Negroid color, but that strain has left its traces in the curly hair!

There is another fear that if we give equality of opportunity to the Negro then in places where the numbers are about equally divided the Negroes will dominate the whites. This is a false fear, coming out of the desire of the white to dominate. If you treat the Negro as a racial being he will respond racially, but if you treat him as a human being he will respond humanly. In our Ashrams in India, where all races live together on the basis of complete equality, we have never known our discussions to divide on the basis of the Westerners on one side and the Indians on the other. Not once in twelve years has that ever happened, though the racial tensions on the outside are very great. The discussions have always divided with the white and the brown radicals on the one side and the white and the brown conservatives on the other. The division between radical and conservative is a division which runs through all races on all questions, for the human mind is made that way. One group would want to conserve values and the other would want to adventure in new ones. That is a healthy division. If the Negro should be treated on the basis of equality of opportunity, the white and the Negro radicals would be on one side of every question and the white and the Negro conservatives on the other. That would be healthy. But now, treated on a racial basis, the Negro and the white react racially. That is unhealthy and dangerous—for both races and for the national life.

This is no longer a local issue; it is a national issue and must be dealt with nationally. To turn the matter over to individual states to be dealt with according to local prejudices is a national blunder. For this nation as a nation gets the blame for the injustices done to the Negro in any local situation. The enemies of democracy pick up every local wrong done anywhere in America and use it against America. Since the nation as a nation bears the blame, the nation must undertake the responsibility to right that wrong. This is something that affects citizens of the United States and not merely local residents of a state.

Therefore let the Christians strive for a solution by four methods: (1) Let there be teaching of the Christian viewpoint concerning man—that he is to be dealt with as a man apart from race and birth and color, as a man "for whom Christ died." Let there be a country-wide campaign of teaching, teaching, teaching. (2) Let there be a nation-wide endeavor to get teaching concerning race appreciation put into our public school system. (3) Let the churches demonstrate a different attitude by each local church's having at least one person of the other race as an honored, respected member of that church as a symbol that Christianity looks on a person as a person. If some white members leave the church on account of this, then let us remember that if that be their mentality they contribute nothing by staying, except to the de-Christianizing of our Christianity. The Christian movement, purified of alien elements, will then go much further into the soul of America than it now does, loaded and crippled into impotence through basic compromises with surrounding culture. (4) Let there be a nation-wide endeavor to get the national government to act to do away with all discriminations to any American citizen, wherever that discrimination may be practiced. (5) If the above steps are ineffective, then Negroes, probably joined by whites, may have to resort to nonviolent non-co-operation, by picking out certain injustices and then, through volunteers trained in nonviolent methods, refusing to obey these specific injustices and taking the consequences of that civil disobedience. This would be an appeal to the conscience of the country.

But the end must not be the ending of discriminations. There must be the endeavor to create out of both parties that new man—the co-operative man. In that situation who will be greatest? The servant of *all!* And that greatness will be beneficial to *all.*

Chapter XIII—

THE GAP BETWEEN OUR FAITH AND OUR GOVERNMENT

PERHAPS THE BIGGEST question confronting those who seriously hold to the Christian faith and who truly love America is: Can the government of this country be Christianized? Not denominationalized, not priest-ridden or pastor-ridden, but can it function in an effective Christian way? Can the Christian faith be put down through the processes of government, and can government in its functionings be the political expression of that faith? That is the question upon which the survival of our democracy depends.

Our democracy will never be broken from without. It may be betrayed from within. For we now see that what matters in democracy is the spirit that animates it, controls it, directs it—and to what ends. When suffrage was given to the people of Ceylon, a woman was seen standing before the ballot box with folded hands in an attitude of saying her prayers to this new god, the Ballot Box. We once did that. The word "democracy" was the magic word which, when whispered into the ears of oppressed peoples, would cure all their ills. We now see that the ballot box is an instrument, and only an instrument, for registering convictions. Those convictions may be good or bad; so the ballot box may be the instrument of good or evil. It all depends upon the enlightened and trustable moral character which comes to that ballot box. The ballot box is simply the registrant of character. If the character that comes to that ballot box is weak, selfish, or uninformed, then the resultant government will be weak, selfish, and uninformed.

Then the government cannot be Christianized until the people are Christianized? That is true in one sense and yet not true in another. For the great changes in American life have come through minorities. Lecky, the historian, says: "The American Revolution, like most others, was the work of an energetic minority who succeeded in committing an undecided and fluctuating majority to courses for which they had little love, and leading them step by step to a position from which it was impossible to recede." That minority had a cause—the cause of freedom. Any determined minority can change any situation, provided it has a cause and is willing to pay a price to see that cause put into operation. Someone has said, "Five per cent of the people think; ten per cent of the people think they think; and the rest of the people would rather die than think." It is that five per cent with a cause, and disciplined beyond the rest, that can change any situation. And the Christians have the cause! *The* cause! They can therefore change the character of our government if they decide to do so.

On two conditions:

First, they must cease the appalling political aloofness and indifference that turns over the government of our country into the hands of less than the best, often into the hands of the worst. The best talent of our country has been drained off into business, where the monetary rewards are greater than in politics. On the whole, with fine exceptions, second-rate men have gone into public office. The political life of America has sagged below the level of the average best from which political leaders should be drawn. This is serious. Lord Bryce, a friend of our democracy, says that our great cities are a more serious threat to America than was slavery. These great cities have fallen into the hands of political machines which work for their own interests rather than for the public good.

This must be changed if American democracy is to survive. And the Christians, who hold the balance of power, can change it. If the Christians realize their power, and if they learn to unite for great ends, they can change the political life of this country and make it worthy of our great democracy.

How? In two ways. Let Christians cease blind voting. Let them cease to vote Democratic or Republican, and let them vote Christian. By "Christian" I do not mean we should form a separate Christian Party, as is done in some countries—although a "Christian Commonwealth Party" would appeal to millions—but let the Christians stand behind those who will stand for Christian principles in public life. The basic differences between Republican and Democrat have faded out anyway. They are meaningless. Let there be a new alignment: the Christians are those who are for Christian principles, and against those who are not. And when I say "Christian principles" I mean to include in them the great Jewish heritage to which we owe so much.

Kagawa, the great Japanese Christian, says, "There is a heaven America and a hell America." Too long has the "heaven America" been ruled by the "hell America." It is time to change. There is a town in America called Echo.

Most Christians have been living in that town! They have been an echo instead of a voice. They have echoed the surrounding partisanships. Now let them stand for something. Let them be a voice, a living voice that must be heard, and a voice that will be decisive. Herbert Agar, a great newspaper editor, says, "If the Christians return to the basis of their belief, the whole situation is altered." It is. The Christians have the largest number around a single allegiance of any group in this country. They hold the balance of power. Let them exercise it for great ends. Suppose, then, the Christians of this country should politely but firmly and decisively tell the Republican and Democratic parties: "We are through with blindly voting Republican or Democratic. We are going to vote Christian. If you will put up men of Christian character with Christian programs we will vote for them; otherwise we won't. And moreover, if you do not put them up through your party system, we will put them up directly apart from your system."

There has been a separation of church and state in America. And that is right. It was good for the state and for the Church to be separate. In being so each could possess its own soul. But now that this matter is clear, something else has become clear: they have become too separate! The power of living Christian faith has not been turned into the public life of this country to purify and dedicate it to great ends. Only incidentally has religion been a purifying force as it purified individuals going into public life. Now the purification must be deliberate and intentional, not only of individuals, but of policies which those individuals hold. For heretofore purified individuals going into public life have found themselves compelled to respond to the crack of the party whip or get out. Purified individuals were called on to back very unpurified party policies, or have no standing. We must give them standing by solid backing, so they can be free to choose to vote for party policies or against them according as those party policies square with Christian principles.

Christian faith and government processes must come together—not formally but forcefully, not verbally but vitally. The Christian movement can prepare for this new vital alliance by two steps. First by giving up its attitude of aloofness—the attitude that says, "We cannot have anything to do with politics." Can't have anything to do with politics? But politics has something to do with us! It regulates our lives, tells us what to do and not to do, what to eat and not to eat! Abdicate *there?* Then you abdicate at the place where life is vitally determined for millions. Purify politics, or it will stain you! I have said that the phrase that resulted in China's national downfall was the phrase so prevalent in regard to everything public, "It's not on my body"—not my responsibility. Result? That which was on nobody's body was on everybody's body, as universal moral corruption and ruin. That phrase may be our ruin. If it isn't on your body as moral responsibility, it will be on your body as moral and material ruin. The Christian movement must concern itself with governmental processes, for those processes have to do with life, and the sphere of the Christian movement is all life.

Second, the Christian movement must urge young men and women to go into public life. It must insist that the call to put Christian principles into public life is just as sacred a call as to utter them from a pulpit. It should have services of dedication for men and women going into public office. Those elected to public office should go with a sense of mission—a sense that they are being sent by God, and with the backing of the prayers and moral convictions of good people.

In order to train Christian people for public office the seminaries and Christian colleges should offer courses in Christian statesmanship and governmental processes. There is an underlying Christian philosophy of government. One of the outstanding men in the Department of Agriculture of the United States said to me: "I want our officials to feel that there is something more than just raising grains and foodstuffs, that there is a philosophy of life behind it all. Will you speak to us on the Christian philosophy of agriculture?" When someone connected with the State Department heard of this request, the comment was: "I wish you would speak to the officials of the State Department on the Christian philosophy of the state." Those going into public office should see their job in the setting of the Kingdom of God and in the light of eternal principles—those principles made flesh in public life. Nothing, absolutely nothing, is more necessary in the life of American democracy than just this sense of mission to lift the whole thing from the sordid to the sacred. Some few men have caught that vision and possibility and have gone into politics with a sense of divine call and mission. But very many succumb to prevailing attitudes and processes. Why? Because they are bound to a party system, and party politics prevail instead of Christian principles. The way out?

It seems to me that the only way out is for the Christian movement to renounce party allegiance as primary and make the Kingdom of God primary. "Seek ye first the Kingdom of God, . . . and all these things shall be added unto you." But if we seek first the party, then all these things will be subtracted from us—as now. After making the Kingdom first we could say to the parties: "We will stand with you to the degree that you stand for the Kingdom. When you break with that Kingdom, we break with you. For to us the Kingdom loyalty is first, last, and always."

There is this passage which represents the present political position of Christians in this country: "The believers who belonged to the Pharisaic party." (Acts 15:5—Moffatt.) They were "believers," but their conduct was determined more by their allegiance to the Pharisaic party than by their Christian faith. This was shown by a crisis episode in the early Church. (See Acts 15:5-29.) "Believers who belonged to the Pharisaic party" is out of gear—a contradiction. "Believers who belong to the Democratic or to the Republican Party" is also out of gear—a contradiction. They may vote for the Democratic or for the Republican Party when that party stands for Christian principles and outlook, but they do not "belong" to it. They belong to the Kingdom; and they vote for any party, or no party, according as that fits in with their primary allegiance. If the sixty-five million members of the Christian Church in the United States would take that attitude, the political parties would sit up and take notice and would revise their outlook at once. They would have to. If only one out of every five would do it, they would hold the balance of power and turn the public life of this country any way they saw fit.

At its best the Christian Church has been playing a sideline role in public affairs. We mentioned a cartoon showing

Uncle Sam standing on the Ship of State and saying to the religious leaders: "It is your business to keep off from the Ship of State the barnacles of greed, selfishness, and dishonesty." Good, but not good enough. Is the role of Christianity only to keep the barnacles off so that the Ship of State will run smoothly in the direction which others determine? Has Christianity nothing to do with the charting of the course the Ship of State shall take? We will clean barnacles, but only on condition that we also help to determine the goal and to chart the course of the Ship of State.

Does that mean that the Church shall seek to dominate the state and gain political power? Certainly not. The Church, as such, is out of politics, as such; but Christians as Christians are very much in politics, and by concerted action can permeate and determine the public life of our land—and should. For this country desperately needs public cleansing, and it needs consecration. By consecration I mean we must cease to think of our government as something from which to get something and must think of it as something to be dedicated to and served. As someone has said, "America was a cause to be served, but it became a public picnic with free coffee and sandwiches, and let somebody else pick up the mess." The Christians, with their sense of dedication to a cause, can cleanse this attitude of looking on the government as something from which to get something, and can turn it into a cause to be served.

By the application of the principle of making a new man out of both parties, the Christians, now giving first loyalty to political parties, can out of the two political parties form a new man—the Christian man in public life. That new man will gather up in himself the best in the old parties and go beyond each, for his Christianity will give him that plus, that something beyond. That new man is the hope of American life.

Governor Saltonstall of Massachusetts said in a public proclamation regarding Bible Week: "The best things in American life are traceable to the Scriptures." If so—and who can doubt it?—then let the Christian impact no longer be incidental and by indirection. Let it be central and by direct intention. It is the one hope of America. The gap between church and state must be filled. How? By the emergence of the new man out of both parties. That is the only hope.

Chapter XIV—

FEDERAL UNION OF THE CHURCHES AND OF THE NATIONS

IF THE PRINCIPLE of federal union—a new man out of both parties—is inherent both in American democracy and in Christianity, then what about applying it to the churches themselves? If the principle is inherent in the Christian faith, then the churches need not hesitate to take it for fear it would copy a state organization. For the Christian faith was the first to uncover and announce this universal principle. So when it comes to that principle, it comes to its own.

The American churches have achieved analysis; they have not achieved synthesis. The stage of analysis was inevitable and necessary. When the Christian faith was transplanted from Europe and put in a new setting, then new values were discovered. With the freshness of the outlook of pioneers, the Christians went to the Bible and discovered emphases neglected in the European expression of Christianity. Around those neglected emphases denominations grew up. These once-neglected truths have thus been preserved and propagated by separate denominations, but now they have seeped over from those denominations and have become a part of the total life of the Church. They are a part of the general heritage. We of the different denominations are reading the same books and singing the same hymns and are now closer together in mind and spirit than in organization. The ideas that unite us are infinite; those that divide us are infinitesimal. We are united at the center and divided at the margin. I have found in my Round Table Conference that when the Christians drop down beneath the level of organization to the level of experience, there they share a common life—the life of Christ. They are united in the deepest thing in life, namely in life itself. The Christians are at once the most united people on earth and the most divided—united in life and divided in organization. How can we express in organization that unity which we really have in life?

There are three possibilities: (1) amalgamation, (2) federation, (3) federal union. If we wait for all the churches to unite by amalgamation, I'm afraid we shall wait till doomsday. I cannot visualize the High-churchman and the Baptist or the Quaker being able to accept the same type of church government. I don't know what Quakers would do with bishops, and I don't know what bishops would do with Quakers! And yet we must have both the High-churchman and the Quaker in the union. Besides, even if you should succeed in jamming all into one ecclesiastical mold, I fear that the divisions would begin all over again, for portions of the union would probably feel their truth was not sufficiently emphasized. Then the divisions would begin again. Complete amalgamation, wiping out names and pasts of various denominations and having all sign on the dotted line accepting the same church polity and government, is a mirage. It won't happen.

Those who insist on one type of ordination, namely episcopal ordination, as the basis of union are laying the foundation not for ultimate union but for ultimate division. For in insisting on one type of ordination they are excluding those who cannot accept that ordination. In America that means they exclude a majority of Christians. They are therefore providing for disunion rather than union.

Nor will federation do. For in federation the constituent bodies make the great refusal—the refusal to surrender sovereignty for the sake of union. To refuse that is to break oneself on the law, "Whosoever will save his life shall lose it." Only those who "lose" life will find it again. That is absolute for individuals and for groups. Federation isn't enough.

The third possibility is federal union. In federal union would be avoided the totalitarianism of complete amalgamation on the one side, and the individualism of federation on the other side. The truth in individualism and the truth in totalitarianism would be summed up in a third something beyond each—a new man out of both parties, federal union. Moreover in federal union the two instincts in man would be satisfied—the desire for union with the whole and the desire for local self-expression. Refusal to fulfill those two desires will end in conflict and instability. Specifically what would federal church union mean?

1. There would be one Church and only one Church—"The Church of Christ in America." The present separate churches would cease to exist as separate churches. The great renunciation would be made for the sake of the union—and incidentally for the sake of the churches themselves.

2. Under "The Church of Christ in America" there would be branches—branches of the one church: "The Baptist

Branch of the Church of Christ in America," "The Episcopal Branch," "The Lutheran Branch," "The Nazarene Branch," and so on down the line.

3. Within these branches there would be local self-government—states' rights, as it were. If the Baptist Branch wanted adult immersion, then it could be free to have it. But it wouldn't impose its mode and conditions on the rest as the price of union. The Episcopal Branch could have bishops and could take any view of the episcopacy it deemed best, but it wouldn't impose bishops on the rest as the price of union. The Baptists and the Quakers inherently could not accept bishops without destroying the basis of their existence.

We would not ask any branch to sacrifice any truth, or worth-while emphasis on a truth, in coming into the union.

4. Over these branches would be a "General Assembly of the Church of Christ in America." This General Assembly would be made up of delegates pro rata from the branches. It would be the sovereign body, with powers granted to it by a constitutional convention, and amended as the General Assembly might from time to time deem best.

Under the General Assembly would be the state, county, and city assemblies. In the county and city assemblies the questions of overlapping, duplication, and competition in local situations could be dealt with. Since all the local churches would belong to the same church, all point about local competition would be taken away—the church shouldn't compete with itself. This local competition and duplication could be dealt with in two ways: amalgamation of local churches and division of territory between branches.

The General Assembly would deal with matters relating to the whole church—evangelism, education, weekday religious education, the Christian faith and industry and race, the Christian faith and the state, and the Christian faith and international affairs.

5. In each country there would be a national expression of the universal Church—"The Church of Christ in China," "The Church of Christ in Britain," "The Church of Christ in India," "The Church of Christ in Mexico," and so on. Each national expression would embody the peculiar genius of that nation and make it available to the rest of us for our enrichment.

Over these national expressions would be "The World Assembly of the Church of Christ." This assembly would be made up of delegates from the national general assemblies and would deal with the world-wide expression of the Church and its interests. It could speak the mind of the Church on great international issues. Speaking for the whole Church, it would be listened to. Suppose it could speak now in the midst of a wavering world!

6. Within each branch there would be freedom to make any conditions, or no conditions, for the exchange of members and ministers and for intercommunion. Probably ninety-five per cent of the constituent branches would at once be willing to have intercommunion and free exchange of members and ministers. The remaining five per cent we would leave to time and to the Spirit of God. They would be within the stream of union, and the tendency would be to break down remaining barriers.

7. If any two or more branches should desire to amalgamate, they could be free to do so. There would be that

many fewer branches in "The Church of Christ in America." Thus under federal union, union by amalgamation could go on as far as it could go. It would probably reach certain limits. But union by amalgamation could proceed within federal union.

8. In regard to the doctrinal basis of the federal union, we could take the basis that Jesus laid down. When Peter made the great confession, "Thou art the Christ, the Son of the living God," Jesus said, "Blessed art thou, Simon Barjona: for flesh and blood hath not revealed it unto thee, but my Father which is in heaven. . . . Thou art Peter, and upon this rock I will build my church." What was the "rock" upon which the Church was to be built? On Peter the man? If so, it was a wobbly rock, for in a verse below Jesus says to Peter, "Get thee behind me, Satan." Then the "rock" must be the confession that Peter made. The rock upon which the Christian Church is founded is the rock of the confession that Jesus is "the Christ, the Son of the living God." That is literally the rock which is beneath all the churches, for that confession is distinctive and distinguishes a *Christian* Church.

Then any branch that will confess that Jesus is "the Christ, the Son of the living God" is on the "rock." We ask no more; we can ask nothing less. In that confession the germ of all Christian faith is to be found. We are safe in taking Christ's own basis instead of elaborate statements built up by man. The existing Christian churches almost one hundred per cent could accept that basis.

9. What about the Roman Catholic and the Greek Orthodox churches? If the Roman Catholic or any other body will acknowledge itself as a "branch" of the Christian

Church, then the door is open. We could have "The Roman Catholic Branch of the Church of Christ in America." If the Roman Catholic would be unwilling to make that acknowledgment, then we do not close the door. The door is aways open—*on that basis.*

10. That leads me to say that if any church is unwilling to acknowledge itself as a branch, and others as branches, of the Christian Church and still talks union, then the matter is plain: that church does not want union; it wants absorption of the others into itself. I need not add that I am not interested in any one denomination's absorbing the rest. In the first place, it won't happen; and in the second place, if it did happen, it would impoverish the corporate expression of Christianity. For no denomination has the Truth; the Truth is in Christ who is *the* Truth. What we hold is truths more or less approximating him who is the Truth. We therefore need the pooled truths of all the various emphases so that these pooled truths may more or less approximate him who is the Truth.

11. The inner structure of this world organization has already been laid within the Christian churches. In America we have the Federal Council of the Churches of Christ in America. This Council, now only a council with advisory powers, could be made into the executive of "The General Assembly of the Church of Christ in America." From an advisory body it could become executive, functioning in between meetings of the General Assembly and carrying out its decisions. In Britain, India, China, Mexico, and other countries there have been formed National Christian Councils. Each of these could be made the executive of the General Assembly of its particular country. Moreover there has

been in process of formation a World Council of Churches. This World Council could become the executive of "The World Assembly of the Church of Christ." Then, again, within our cities and counties we have the variously named church councils. These councils, from the city- to the world-wide, could be transformed into executives with little upset and confusion. Thus we see that the inner keel has already been laid for federal union.

The question is raised whether federal union is real union or only a federation—an organization instead of an organism. The reply is: Is a real marriage a federation or a union? It is a union, but it is a federal union. The partners have a common name, but each has a separate name; they have a common life, and yet each has a separate life; they are one, but they are also two. The highest loyalty is to the union, but they have a subsidiary loyalty to themselves. Within the area of that supreme loyalty each is free to express himself or herself. The two instincts of desire for union with the whole and desire for local self-expression are satisfied in a real marriage. Federal union of the churches almost completely parallels union in marriage—a common name and a separate name, a common life and a separate life, highest loyalty to the union and a subsidiary loyalty to the branch, the two instincts of desire for union and desire for self-expression satisfied. If federal union completely parallels marriage, then it is union, for marriage is the closest bond that human beings are capable of having.

Is federal union in the United States a union or a federation? It is a union. We are united as Americans; there is a supreme loyalty to the union; but within the area of that supreme loyalty there is a subsidiary loyalty to the individual state. This gives satisfaction of the instincts of union with the whole and of local self-expression. Federal union is real union—the only union possible among equals.

The greatest difficulty will probably come from vested interests, for federal union would ultimately mean the merging of a great many duplicating boards. But that such a merging of boards—with each denomination duplicating all the machinery of all the rest—ought to take place is obvious. Such duplication is wasteful and unnecessary and inefficient.

If the Christian churches of America should unite in federal union, it would be the fulfilling of the genius of American democracy with its central idea of *"E pluribus unum,"* and it would also fulfill the central genius of the Christian faith with its teaching of the new man out of both parties. We would fulfill both. But the Christian conception of the new man out of both parties is prior. Therefore we are not copying a secular government; we are continuing an inherent conception, and bringing it to flower and fruit.

The next great step is for the churches to unite, and the only feasible basis seems to be federal union. For federal union can be accomplished *now.*

If the churches should unite in a federal union, then they would be fitted to lead in something that is emerging inevitably in the world situation—a federal union of the nations. When Clarence Streit wrote *Union Now,* I was an early approver—with reservations. I believe profoundly in it, for it seemed to corroborate the conception of federal union for the churches which had come to me several years before. But I would have amended Streit's scheme, for its original nucleus of fifteen nations included only white. You cannot have an all-white nucleus of a world federal union, for the whites are only one third and the colored are two thirds. The colored races must be taken in at the very inception as an integral part of the whole.

When *Union Now* was amended and it was proposed that the world federation begin with an Anglo-American federal union, then I was unable to accept it. Psychologically it would be impossible for the rest of the world to come into an Anglo-American union, for the Anglo-Americans would give it shape and would dominate it, consciously or unconsciously. Suppose the Germanic races were to form such a union and invite us into it, could we enter? Or suppose Japan, China, and India were to form such a union. Again, could we enter? To ask the question is to answer it. It would by psychologically impossible.

The only possible federal union of the world must begin with representatives of all races in the original nucleus. That will take away all suspicion of one group's dominating another.

That we must come to a world federal union there is not the slightest doubt in my mind. It is inevitable. It is our collective destiny. We may not do it now—we may not be big enough—but we will have to do it sometime or perish through mutual strife. "Co-operate or perish!" is written across the future. Balances of power, imperialisms, Leagues of Nations, isolationisms are dead conceptions. They have failed. The League, which was the best conception, failed because each nation refused the surrender of any sovereignty for the sake of a union. Each saved its life and lost it—lost it in universal strife. The League tried the impossible—to have a world brotherhood out of an unwillingness to surrender the self to something larger than itself. Only as you lose yourself in something beyond yourself do you find yourself again. The nations will never find themselves as harmonious, contributing, progressive entities unless they lose a part of their sovereignty in a federal union. If two people about to be married should say, "We will set up a union, a marriage, but neither one of us must be called on to surrender any of the self to that union; each self will be sovereign, but we will have a marriage," the marriage would end as the League ended—in strife. This law of saving your life by losing it is as deeply written into the constitution of reality as the law of gravitation is written into the physical universe—and is as inescapable. Upon that law men will build or break.

If federal union of the nations is our collective destiny, then it is the national destiny of America to help form that federal union, for it is but the flowering of something inherent in our central genius. And if that is our American destiny, it is the destiny of the churches of America to lead America to fulfill her world destiny of helping to create a world federal union. The churches themselves can do this by demonstrating in themselves that federal union at work. Without that demonstration the churches' leadership will be verbal instead of vital. For a divided Church in a divided world has little moral authority. Christians of America, unite! You have your greatest world opportunity for the reshaping of the world in doing so. You have nothing to lose except your dividing walls!

Chapter XV

THE EMERGING AMERICAN
INTERPRETATION

WE HAVE LOOKED at the universal Christ embodying the universal order, the Kingdom of God. This universal Christ stands in silent judgment upon the American interpretation of him and his Kingdom. There is a painting of Christ standing silently watching Justice as she holds the scales— he judges even Justice. So the real Christ stands judging our interpretations. What have we made of him? Is our interpretation anything like the real thing?

The first judgment must be favorable. With all its faults the Church is the best institution in American life. Out of the Christian movement came democracy itself. Its faith in God gave a faith in man, for you cannot believe in man long unless you believe in something more than man, something that gives permanence, worth, meaning, ultimate goal to man. That something is Someone—God, who is the ground of our faith in man and his possibilities.

Moreover the Christian movement has been a cleansing moral movement. It has been the greatest character-forming movement in our national life. This is important, for the whole outer structure of life rests upon that imponderable something called character. If the character breaks, the confidence breaks; and if the confidence breaks, the country breaks. The Christian movement sustains the country by remaking and sustaining the character of its citizens. It is no mere chance that ninety-five per cent of the people who belong to the service clubs of America—clubs which hold within them the cream of the business and professional life of our cities—are members of some church. Only about fifty per cent of those who are members of churches are really working at it, and yet even though the influence is by indirection there is a cleansing impulse that makes men more dependable and honorable and upright. As someone put it, "Being a Presbyterian may not save you from sin, but it takes the joy out of it." Men connected with churches may sin, but they do it with hesitation; they cannot sin with the stops out. Someone has facetiously defined an Episcopalian as "one who believes it is wrong to sin during Lent." That is a travesty, of course, but even on that low plane there is something introduced into life that has a moral foothold which influences the whole of life. It is no mere chance that while one out of every five marriages in the United States now goes to pieces on the rocks in a divorce court, only one out of fifty marriages among church members ends up in divorce. Evidently the Christian faith helps people to live together—if not "on account of," then "in spite of"! Again, it is no mere chance that a judge said that of four thousand cases of delinquency among youth, only thirteen of them were among youth who attended church or Sunday school. The dean of girls in a public school said that the three causes of delinquency were "poverty, broken homes, and a lack of attendance on church or Sunday school." The Christian faith produces better character.

Again, the Christian faith sensitizes people—makes them

care. And it makes them care in larger and larger circles, and across more and more boundary lines of class and race. As I write this, I am in a Japanese Relocation Center. A caustic critic of Christianity among the evacuees said: "I have been a very severe critic of religion, but I'm afraid I'll have to change my mind. The Christians are the only people who care. They have shown in this crisis that their religion makes them care." Incidentally, may I say that among the evacuees themselves the Christians have proved that they can take it—can take it better than people who have no sustaining faith or who have a non-Christian faith. The superintendent of one of these camps said to me: "Christianity has proved right here before our eyes that it gives people power to live and to live happily and usefully under very adverse conditions. The Christians stand up under this far better than others. Others are embittered by what they feel is injustice, while the Christians have learned to take hold of injustice and make something out of it. They use it."

A month or so after the war broke out I was in a mass meeting in Denver when a Japanese girl was announced to sing. I held my breath. This was war; how would the people take it? She sang, "How beautiful upon the mountains are the feet of him that bringeth good tidings, that publisheth peace"; and she sang it beautifully. When she finished, although it was a religious meeting and there had been of course no applause, yet that audience broke out in a spontaneous wave of applause that was deep and sincere. The feeling was: "She is a Christian; we are Christians. We are not at war; we are one in Christ, where there is no East or West." Only in a Christian church could that happen in wartime. An American airman, decorated with the Order of the Purple Heart, was shot down near the Solomon Islands. He swam for nine hours with a broken leg, landed on an island where he was taken care of by native Christians for a month. They gave him of their simple best. He entered their services and sang their hymns with them. He said to me: "I can see why you are a missionary. I went out to the South Seas to bomb, but I'd like to go back as a missionary to people like that. They were wonderful to me." Christians had discovered each other. A Japanese airman was shot down over Nanking and was taken care of in a Chinese hospital. After some days he said to the nurses: "I am puzzled. I was told you were barbarians with no culture and we would have to give you ours. But you attend to me kindly and graciously—me, an enemy. What makes you do it?" "We are Christians," replied the nurses. "Christians?" exclaimed the airman. "Why, so am I! When I was sent over to bomb defenseless people I felt I couldn't do it, so I dropped my bombs in an open field outside the city." And, sure enough, they found the pockmarks of the bombs in the open field. Christians had found each other!

In Nanking, in the South Seas, in a Christian church in America, across all boundaries, Christians are held together in unbreakable bonds—the only bonds holding across the chasms of hate and prejudice caused by war.

The Christian movement has been creative—creating education (ninety-five per cent of the higher educational institutions of the United States arose out of Christian denominations), creating the humanitarian movements, creating character, making people care beyond their own interests, producing a brotherhood across race and class. With all its faults the Christian Church is the best-serving institution on earth. It has many critics but no rivals in the work of human redemption. It has filled the earth with schools, hospitals, orphan and leper asylums, agricultural institutions —in fact with every type of institution for the purposes of human uplift. No other institution has done anything like it. If you should wipe out the Christian Church today, we would have to produce some other movement like it to take its place. "The Church is a crusading body, intent on creating a new divine society on earth." If so, it is indispensable. Someone has put it this way: "The churches do three things: First, they teach men to worship. Worship is basic self-direction. Second, they teach people to read the Bible. The Bible contains those basic truths which, if acted on, make human association possible. Third, churches create in people a concern for other people."

The first judgment on the Christian movement must be favorable.

All of this is true concerning the Christian movement; and yet the universal Christ, embodying the universal Order, speaks to the American interpretation of himself and his Kingdom and pronounces loving judgment on it in almost the identical words used of the church at Ephesus: "I know thy works, and thy labor, and thy patience, and how thou canst not bear them which are evil. . . . Nevertheless I have somewhat against thee, because thou hast left thy first love." (Rev. 2:2, 4.) Not thy first American Christian love, but thy first Christian love; the Christianity of America differs fundamentally from the Christianity of Christ.

The first fundamental lack of American Christianity is that it lacks the Kingdom content so utterly characteristic of the Christianity of Christ. We must remind ourselves that with Jesus the Kingdom was the starting point, the master light of all his seeing, the framework in which all his teaching was set. It was to be sought "first," not merely in loyalty, but in emphasis—the divine totalitarianism demanding complete obedience in the total life, here and hereafter.

This has not been our emphasis. The Kingdom has been marginal; the Church has been central. Hence the Church has not been the embodiment of the new Order; it has been an aggregation of worshiping individuals. It has therefore lacked universal relevancy; people could disregard it without feeling they were disregarding a universal fact and issue. The Church has not embodied the Cause, and hence has not had the significance of that Cause. When the Church makes itself the cause, it falls flat on the conscience of the world. It matters much as to the framework within which repentance is demanded. Jesus made the Kingdom of God the framework of repentance: "Repent: for the Kingdom of Heaven is at hand." But suppose I should come and say, "Repent, for I am at hand." You would burst out laughing: "Who are you, in the light of which we should repent?" Again, suppose I should say, "Repent, for the Ashram is at hand"; then again you would smile. And if I should say, "Repent, for the Church is at hand," you would probably laugh, as an audience once did in India when I said just that. But if I say, "Repent, for the Kingdom of God is at hand," then you do not laugh; you inwardly tremble, for you feel that you are being confronted with God's absolute Order with its absolute demand. The Church has lacked the awful authority of speaking in the name of a Cause beyond itself and yet embodied in itself. If it works from the relativism of itself to the relativisms of the hour, it will have little or no effect. But if it confronts men with God's Order embodied in God's Person, then its message falls upon the souls of men with authority.

When the Church has dealt with the Kingdom, it has dealt with it in about four ways: (1) It has pushed it into the inner recesses of the soul as personal mystical experience, or (2) it has pushed it beyond the borders of this life into heaven as a heavenly collective experience. Between the inner personal mystical experience and the heavenly collective experience whole areas are left out—the economic, the political, the racial, the international—these are all left unredeemed. The totalitarians of the hour have stepped into the resulting vacuum and have said, "Keep your mystical experience now and your collective experience hereafter in heaven; we will take over the rest of the areas of life and control them." The Church has therefore been helpless and confused before the totalitarianisms of the day, for it has lost its own totalitarianism, the Kingdom. Only as it regains the Kingdom will it speak with planet-encompassing authority.

(3) When the Church has put the Kingdom into human affairs, it has put it in as an apocalyptic hope at the return of Christ. That takes it out of the realm of immediate relevancy as an immediate issue. It is a hope. The New Testament does teach an apocalyptic coming of the Kingdom, but it also teaches a present coming by gradualism: "The Kingdom of Heaven is like to a grain of mustard seed. . . . The Kingdom of Heaven is like unto leaven." Some pick out one set of passages, the apocalyptic; and others pick out the other set, the gradualistic. But I cannot do that; for both

are integral parts of the account, and neither one can be picked out without disrupting the account. Then I shall take both, for I need both. The gradualism gives me my task—I can be the agent of the coming of the Kingdom now. The apocalyptic gives me my hope—my hope that the last word in human affairs will be spoken by God, perhaps suddenly, and that last word will be victory. But the American Church has not achieved the synthesis of those two methods of the coming of the Kingdom, and one without the other is barren. To emphasize the apocalyptic coming of the Kingdom only is to run into spiritual crystal gazing, trying to peer into the future through the crystal of every passing event. On the other hand, to dismiss the apocalyptic coming and see only gradual permeation is to live a human-event-bound life. The lift that comes from a chastened belief in the divine intervention is taken away. God intervened in a personal incarnaton—a sudden intervention at the end of a long preparation—and he may intervene again in personal and collective incarnation in the coming of the Kingdom. And that may be sudden.

(4) We have reduced the Kingdom to the coming of social reform. We have reduced this majestic coming of the Kingdom to progress in social justice and amenities. When we have emphasized the gradualism, we have made it into social reform—a building of the Kingdom. Nowhere in the New Testament are we told to "build the Kingdom." It is already built "from the foundation of the world," built into the nature of reality. You "see," "enter," "proclaim," "suffer for" the Kingdom, but never "build" it. For the Kingdom is not a relativism to be built, but an absolute to be accepted, submitted to, obeyed. The reason the emphasis on

the Kingdom by earnest men of a generation ago lacked lasting power was because it was largely identified with social reform. Not entirely, of course. But in large measure it lacked eternal meanings and eternal authority. Then came the European reaction against "American activism," and the Kingdom in this European reaction was made entirely apocalyptic and future.

The time has now come for a synthesis of these two views. American activism is the thesis of which European apocalypticism is the antithesis, and now out of the clash of opposites the synthesis—the Kingdom itself—must come. Out of the two a new man must arise, "so making peace." If gradualism conquers there will be no peace, and if apocalypticism conquers there will be no peace; but if they both change, then the truth in each will be gathered up into a third something, the new man, the real Kingdom. That will make peace. The Kingdom by gradualism is a half-truth; the Kingdom by apocalypticism is a half-truth; but the Kingdom by gradualism and apocalypticism is nearer the whole truth. That synthesis will open the door for wholehearted Christian participation in present world reconstruction, and also for faith in "the regeneration when the Son of Man shall sit in the throne of his glory."

The revivification of American Christianity waits upon the rediscovery of the Kingdom of God content not as a gradualism or an apocalypticism but as both. When the American Church rediscovers the Kingdom of God in its full meaning, there will be a spiritual awakening covering all areas of life. Without that majestic conception gripping all its activities and loyalties, the Church sinks into petty irrelevancies and marginal issues; it does not confront the whole of life with a total demand for a total obedience in the total life.

While in a city in Mexico I occupied a rooftop room. A dog with a tremendous sense of his importance would run around the parapet of a building opposite and bark at the traffic below. The traffic moved on as before, but the dog after his strident barking would go and lie down with a great sense of satisfaction that he was directing human affairs from his lofty parapet pulpit. After a rest he would resume his periodic barking at the traffic. "That," I said to myself, "is the Christian Church standing on its lofty pulpit parapets hurling irrelevant anathemas at the traffic of human events." That traffic moves on as before, directed by policemen—representatives of the state—and impelled by economic motives. The state and materialism, not the Church, direct the flow of life. For the Church without the Kingdom emphasis has no real message either to the state or to material relationships; so it stands on lofty pulpit parapets hurling irrelevant dogmatics at the passing show. It rests for a week and then resumes parapet pronouncements on the following Sunday. That, I know, is a travesty on the Church, but it has enough truth in it to make it sting.

"We have inoculated the world with a mild form of Christianity so that it is now proof against the real thing." Christianity with the Kingdom-now emphasis is revolutionary—totally revolutionary—and we have made it resolutionary. We pass a resolution and pass by the revolution. Christianity without the Kingdom-now emphasis is a dead issue. It can be dismissed with a wave of the hand, or turned over to the women and the children.

The Emerging American Interpretation

The thing that impresses me as I go about American church life is its dullness. It is not popping with newness. You can anticipate what it will do. A divine creative activity does not seem to be working at its heart. In Canada there is a sign on a dirt road, "Choose your rut, for you'll be in it for the next twenty miles." So much of the church life is grooved, rutted. It is anticipatable—so smooth and regular and grooved—"faultily faultless, icily regular, and splendidly null." It does not "turn the world upside down"; it conforms to the world, fits in, is an echo instead of a living voice. Its gospel is often as equivocal and meaningless as the advertisement, "This preparation is recommended to cure anything for which it is beneficial"—which says exactly nothing.

In Canada I said to a group: "You are among the most lovable people on earth. But we don't expect any leadership from Canada. You are an echo. Canada echoes the Empire, and the Church echoes Canada." That can be said of much of the American Church—it echoes American life.

Jesus said: "Every scribe who has become a disciple of the Realm of heaven is like a householder who produces what is new." (Matt. 13:52—Moffatt.) Even if you are as dull and copyist as a scribe, who created nothing, you will produce "what is new" provided you become "a disciple" to the Kingdom of God. If the Church had become a disciple to the Kingdom of God—had made it its central study and loyalty and message—then it would be so relevant as to be inescapable in every area of life; then it would have something eternally new to bring forth in every situation. Without that universal relevancy and eternal newness pressing upon every situation—personal and collective—and bringing crisis and conversion everywhere, the Church sinks back into irrelevant niceties, and the minister becomes "a mild-mannered person trying to persuade mild-mannered people to become more mild-mannered." And the services become insufferably dull. The movement which was to make the conscience of the world uncomfortable now turns in on itself and seeks its own comfort—mental and physical.

A bishop preached a stirring sermon on "nor the soft . . . shall inherit the Kingdom of God." (I Cor. 6:9-10—taking the Greek word for "effeminate" in its literal sense.) It was a stirring call to self-sacrifice and hardness. The minister at the close said: "We are now going to take up a collection for something that will appeal to you all; we are going to take up a collection to put in new cushions." "The soft shall not inherit the Kingdom"—"we are going to put in new cushions"! And the tragedy was that not one person smiled. It seemed the natural and Christian thing to do—to tax themselves to make themselves more comfortable! Jesus said: "When an unclean spirit leaves a man, it roams through dry places in search of ease." (Luke 11:24—Moffatt.) If "in search of ease" is the sign of an unclean spirit, then modern Christianity is vastly unclean. It has become infected with the virus of modern desire for refinements of comfort: bumpless springs in cars going nowhere in particular; rightly shaped pews for spineless backs; soft, purring sermons for itching ears. A label on a mattress says, "Comfort first." That is a label attached to many a church building and program. "Seek ye first comfort, and all these things shall be added," has replaced, "Seek ye the first the Kingdom of God, . . . and all these things shall be added." The result? Have we caught the people by offering them a comfortable pew and a comfortable gospel? We haven't. The fastest-growing sect in America is "The Seventh-Day Absentists." The masses know reality—especially the younger generation; they can sniff reality from afar; their noses are acutely sensitive to it. And they sense that *this* is different from New Testament Christianity.

A country minister in preaching a funeral sermon said, "The corpse has been a member of this church for twenty years." Lots of corpses are members, and moreover very often the whole proceeding is dead. Behind a minister's head while he preached could be seen a stained-glass window with the inscription, "He being dead yet speaketh." The dead are burying the dead. Some church services are mechanical, as mechanical as a sign in a restaurant which flashed on periodically, "God bless America." "That is America's modern equivalent to a Buddhist prayer wheel," I remarked to a friend.

A minister said to me, "I can't put an amplifying system into my church, for it only amplifies the echoes." Preaching in many modern pulpits is only amplifying the echoes: the echoes of outside prevailing culture are brought into the church; religious tones are put to them; and then they are amplified. Modern pagan culture cracks its whip and says: "Smoke! It's smart," and forthwith a flock of church women begin to puff—"Everybody does it, you know." "It's smart to drink," and church members cave in to an advertising slogan. "If the church members of this city did not patronize the taverns, they couldn't keep open," said a detached observer. A committeewoman of the national Y.W.C.A. said, "I must go a day ahead of the Y.W.C.A. Conference, so I can get my drinking over before the conference begins."

She did, and in doing so pulled down a struggling young woman battling with drink. A group of church officials took out a fine, spiritual young parish visitor on Saturday night for supper at a night club, presumably as a preparation for Sunday morning worship. A cartoon says, "If you knew where I was Saturday night, you would know why I am not in church on Sunday morning." Said a church member in glee, "I took the hymn number on Sunday morning and won fifty dollars on it." The distinction between those inside the church and those outside is breaking down. And mind you: if there is no outer difference between the Church and the world, there is no inner.

Moreover, and deeper, the racial and economic attitudes of the outside world have invaded the churches; the echoes of those attitudes are taken into the Church and amplified. Instead of producing a Christian culture and society of its own, the Church has been invaded and conquered by prevailing pagan culture. How many American churches have got as far as the church at Antioch, where "Simeon the Black" was a prophet and teacher and laid his hands upon Saul and Barnabas to ordain them? How many churches even have a colored person as a member? "If you take in that colored person as a member I'll leave," said an official. On which another official remarked, "If you don't take him in some of us will leave, for a church that is founded on a racial and class snobbery isn't worth staying in. Besides, if this member does go, then it will be no loss, for with that spirit he was never really in." That should be the general attitude. I fear it is the exception.

As the racial attitudes of the outside world have invaded the Church, so have the economic. On the face of it you would think that the Church would be predisposed by its underlying teachings and spirit to sponsor and demonstrate a co-operative order where the commandment, "Thou shalt love thy neighbor as thyself," would be operative—a society of mutual aid. Instead we have taken over and given religious sanction to an order which says, "Thou shalt love thyself"—a society of mutual suppression, a dog-eat-dog economy. "Our society is in an organized and legalized attempt to get the better of one another." And yet the Church has not stood, on the whole, for basic change; it has stood for amelioration. In a meeting I said: "We must have a new order; everybody must work, and there must be no parasites." A woman's voice called out a clear "Amen." I nearly fainted! That Amen was historic; it wasn't the usual place of the Amen. Let that Amen grow into a chorus of conviction and there is hope. But at that statement the ordinary member has substituted in place of an Amen an "Oh Yeah?" He has an inner skepticism of the workability of God's Order. That is the real skepticism in the Christian Church. Hence he is willing to use the Church in the purposes of the old order.

Said a Negro in his prayer: "O Lord, don't let thy servants forget that I live in room 9 at the American Hotel and that I represent the Superior Life Insurance Company." We are not quite that naïve and explicit, but what is the essential difference between that prayer and this billboard advertisement at Easter: "Go to Church on Easter, Florists' Association of ———." Go to church and patronize us! Another: "The Church Is the Foundation of American Life. Go to Church. ——— Coal Company." This is worse: "The Sign of Freedom," an American eagle, then under it a beer glass advertising a certain brand of beer. A billboard sign in an American city pictures a poor family bowing over an empty table, with the prayer caption, "Give us this day our daily bread," and at the bottom the name of a brewing company. Nothing in American life takes more daily bread off the table of the poor than the brewery, and yet they had the effrontery to exploit religion for selfish economic purposes. A selfish acquisitive society will lay hold of anything—patriotism, the Christian faith, anything, and use it for the purposes of personal gain, and feel righteous in doing so. We have commercialized everything, and everything has commercialized us. A radio announcer had just announced in tremulous, impressive tones something like the following: "If you don't get this baking powder you will not rise in this world, and you'll fall flat in the next. Your destiny depends on it!" I said to him, "This is the new evangelism of America. You have all the tones and emotional appeal of the old-time evangelist." He laughingly replied, "If you only knew how we are trained to say these things!" I did; I could see it, feel it.

This commercialization has permeated the whole of American life—including, I am sorry to say, the Church. It has invaded the ministry; and a man's "grade" is often determined, not by his sacrificial service, but by his salary. Behind one pulpit desk I found the collection plates. Many a minister preaches with one eye on the collection plate— how will this affect the collection? He preaches a "collection-plated gospel." Like the soldiers after the resurrection— "They took the money, and did as they were taught"—so many a minister takes the money and does as he is told, trims his gospel to what is acceptable to a commercialized

216

society in order to get its support. In Mexico there is a statue of Christ called "The Christ of the Padlocked Lips." He literally has a heavy padlock on his lips. "Tell him anything and he will not tell it to anyone"—so the worshipers say. In another sense we worship "The Christ of the Padlocked Lips": we will allow him to speak on certain subjects; on others we padlock his lips. He can speak on the individual if he keeps silent on the social. American churches often worship "The Christ of the Padlocked Lips." No wonder the pulpit lacks moral authority in American life. It is too much like American life; it is not greatly different, so its message is not greatly different. A sign on the church bulletin board announcing the sermon topic said, "God's Disappointment. Dr. ——— preaching." A great deal of our preaching must be a disappointment to God, for it is deeply disappointing to man.

Jesus said, "Keep your loins girt and your lamps lit." (Luke 12:35—Moffatt.) Much of American Christianity has its "loins girt"—it is full of fussy activity—but the "lamps" are not "lit." It isn't lifting up a light to men struggling in the darkness of racialism, selfish nationalism, and international conflict. I had spoken on "The Seven Hesitations of American Democracy" to a large service club and expected an unfavorable reaction from this economically conservative group. A businessman came up and said, "I have only one objection to what you said. The Church doesn't preach that." Men despise the Church when it doesn't stand for the Christian viewpoint. Not beginning with the absolute, the Kingdom, it becomes a part of the relativisms of kingdoms of this world. As a consequence it gets its optimisms and its pessimisms from the headlines of the daily newspaper. It goes up and down with them. A sign on a building with windows shattered and doors battered in said, "Pollyanna Club." This age of disillusionment has been hard on surface optimisms; it has shattered the windows and the doors of "Pollyanna Clubs" and has left little but the sign. You cannot keep an optimism unless you begin with an Absolute that remains unshaken amid all human changes—"a Kingdom that cannot be shaken." The Church, having lost that Kingdom emphasis, has taken on the optimisms and pessimisms around it. When situations are hopeful, American theology begins to be hopeful. When situations are dark, then theology begins to stress "demonic forces." American Christianity, standing upon the low hills of relativisms and not on the mount of God's Kingdom, is suffering from "days of low visibility."

In a very important conference of leading churchmen again and again it was stressed that "the first thing is victory"—nothing would come without that. When I had the temerity to suggest that the first thing is not victory—we are not told, "Seek ye first victory, and all these things shall be added unto you," but, "Seek ye first the Kingdom of God, . . . and all these things shall be added unto you"—I seemed unpatriotic, almost blasphemous. Some "ohs" arose, expressing surprise and indignation. And yet we see, as victory draws near, that unless amid that victory we seek first the Kingdom of God that victory will turn to dust and ashes—or worse, it will become the seed plot of a new world war. For "victory" may mean "Vic-Tory"; the Tory mind may take over the victory and turn the whole thing to imperialistic purposes. If so, we will be back again in a worse mess in twenty-five years. The first thing is not "victory." Seek it first and we will do exactly what we did the last time—turn it into a Versailles Treaty and thus lay the foundations of another world conflict.

In a conference a bishop arose and said, "To revive the Church we must get a new slogan. I suggest, 'When in a lurch turn to the Church.' " The Church will not be revived by slogans, but by a change of central loyalty—the central loyalty must be the Kingdom. When in a lurch we cannot turn to the Church unless the Church turns to something beyond itself—the Kingdom. Then we can turn to it with safety and confidence. Another bishop in the same conference facetiously suggested another slogan: "If you are not hatching anything get off the nest." The Church will never hatch anything except disillusionment if it sits on the nest of various relativisms. Let it begin with the Kingdom, and then it will "produce what is new"—and infinitely relevant. Dr. Adolf Keller, the Swiss theologian, dictating to an American stenographer, said, "It will have cosmic meanings," and she wrote, "It will have cosmetic meanings." The only cosmic she knew was cosmetics! Without the starting point of the majestic and eternal meanings of the Kingdom all our cosmics become cosmetics—all our eternal principles become external paint. American Christianity is suffering from a reduced Kingdom and a reduced Christ. We haven't rejected them; we have reduced them. Christ has become a glorified Rotarian, and his majestic gospel has been reduced to "He profits most who serves best." Good, but not good enough.

This was the very thing Jesus warned us against. He knew that we would never be able to reject successfully his gospel; it was too self-verifying. But he did warn about a toned-down gospel—a gospel "insipid," "shaded," "relaxed" (Matt. 5:13, 15, 19—Moffatt), a not-more-than-the-Pharisee type of spiritual life. The editor of *The Christian Century* put it this way: "Many of those most capable of appraising spiritual realities frankly declare that the Christian life of Protestantism is deteriorating under the pervasive influence of secular indifferentism which characterizes modern society. This mood of society is reflected in the Church to such an extent that their inner integration has become attenuated to the point where deep, intelligent Christian commitment is conspicuous by its rarity. An honest appraisal requires the acknowledgment that American Protestantism is spiritually weaker today than at any time in its history." It is; and the reason is that it has no starting point, no Absolute. Since it does not start with the Kingdom of God, it ends by being merged and submerged into the kingdoms of this world.

Since this is true, the Church has failed to bring to a living synthesis differing emphases within itself. Take the fundamentalist-modernist split—for it is a real split, a rift going straight through American Christianity. If the Church had a real grip on the absolute Person embodying the absolute Order, it would have been able to see, in the light of this all-encompassing conception, that both fundamentalism and modernism belong to the Kingdom, "like a householder who produces what is new [modernism] and what is old [fundamentalism] from his stores," and that both emphases are necessary. The fundamentalist is right when he says that something happened in human history in the Incarnation, in the Atoning Death, in the Resurrection, in the coming of the Holy Spirit—something fundamental, and

220

once and for all, that doesn't have to be done over again. He is profoundly right; something happened in human history that divided history into B.C and A.D., and that something was nothing less than the uncovering of the Eternal God—we have seen him in Jesus Christ. Our faith rests upon a fact, not upon a theory—the fact of the Eternal God manifested in Christ, finally and forever. We must hold these convictions, or rather they must hold us. But some modern minds are so open that, like a sieve, they cannot hold a conviction. Hence they do not speak with conviction, nor produce conviction.

But the modernist is also right in insisting that it is not all back there in history; that while Jesus is a final revelation he is also an unfolding revelation; that the truth unfolding through science, through philosophy, through advancing history will not and does not contradict the truth incarnated in Jesus Christ; that we must therefore be unafraid to follow truth wherever it may lead—"Ye shall know the truth, and the truth shall make you free." The following of that truth may, and certainly will, bring one out to a faith in the fundamentals of the gospel, but that faith will be held with an open mind and unafraid soul. Jesus provided for a continuing revelation of himself: "I have yet many things to say unto you, but ye cannot bear them now. Howbeit when he, the Spirit of Truth, is come, he will guide you into all truth: . . . for he shall receive of mine, and shall show it unto you." (John 16:12-14.) "All truth"—the truth in science, in philosophy, in opening events. But that "all truth" is not different from, nor contradictory to, the truth in Christ—"He shall receive of mine, and shall show it unto you." "The Spirit of Truth" is doing that very thing *now*. Christ in a cosmic setting, summing up truths found everywhere, is a larger Christ than the disciples saw—not larger than he was, but larger than they saw. And more light is yet to break out, for while Christ is behind us in history, he is before us eternally unfolding.

Had the Kingdom been the master light of all the seeing of the Church, it could have held these two emphases in a living blend, each cross-fertilizing the other in mutual enrichment. In the half-lights of relativisms fundamentalists and modernists are fighting each other, struggling for the mastery. I am persuaded that if either one wins there will be planned revenge and continuing conflict. The only hope is that we can get each to change and come to a third position beyond each, gathering up the truth in each and eliminating the wrong in each—a new man out of both parties. That will make peace—the peace not of compromise but of comprehension. Then instead of the fundamentalist or the modernist will emerge the Christian.

Again, if the Church will set Christianity in the framework of the Kingdom, it will probably be able to bring varying denominational emphases into a living blend; for none of them has the truth—they hold truths about the Truth, but all are a part of a Kingdom which fulfills them all and goes beyond them all. Church union set in the framework of denominational relativisms becomes a tug of war as to which denominational truth is recognized as uppermost, and therefore church union becomes impossible. But church union set in the framework of the Kingdom puts each denomination in its place, not as *the* Truth, but as a phase of something beyond itself. Church union is an almost inevitable corollary of the rediscovery of the Kingdom.

Some goldfish were taken from a bowl and put into a pond. At first, accustomed to confinement, they swam only in tiny circles about the size of their bowl, and only gradually did they discover that the whole pond was theirs. We who have been used to swimming in the close confines of denominational loyalty and life are almost afraid to realize the gracious truth that the whole pond of the Kingdom is ours—that all the truths discovered by all the groups are a part of our heritage, and that we can take them gladly and joyously and share with others what we have discovered. At first we will hug our particular truth as *the* Truth, but a larger consciousness will dawn upon us. It has been found that goldfish will be small and stunted if raised in a bowl, but will grow very much larger if put into a pond. Christians grown in the small confines of denominational bowls remain small—small compared to what they would be if grown in the pond of the larger Christian consciousness.

A girl of twelve went to her first young people's summer camp. She refused to go unless she could take her favorite doll along. Her parents wisely consented, knowing at the same time the incongruity of a doll at a summer camp. The first day the girl hugged her doll to her bosom and then finding that no other young person had a doll, she quietly put hers aside and transferred her affections from the doll to the fellowship of the group. When we come into federal union of the churches we will wisely allow adolescent Christians to bring their denominational dolls along—names, forms, emphases, knowing that when they once discover the fellowship of the Kingdom they will quietly lay aside these dolls and enter this grown-up and mature fellowship. The transference of affection will be made. The dolls had their place in awakening loyalty and love, but that loyalty and love must be transferred to the supreme loyalty of the Kingdom. A child that does not make that transference and persists in keeping doll affection is suffering from arrested development. American Christianity is suffering from arrested development. In its hesitation to make the transference to a larger loyalty it shows it is still in a childhood stage, has never grown up.

The three stages of human growth are: dependence—childhood; independence—adolescence; interdependence—maturity. The American Church is in its adolescent stage; it is insisting on its own denominational separateness and independence. That stage was necessary; adolescence is a part of human development where the child sets up an independent life, makes his own decisions. But if the child, cutting loose from his mother's apron strings and setting up an independent personality, stops there, he becomes self-centered, immature, an arrested personality. For his own sake he must pass on to interdependence. Dependence is the thesis of which independence is the antithesis, and then out of the clash of opposites emerges the synthesis, interdependence, which gathers up the truth in dependence and the truth in independence into a living blend—the new man out of both parties.

The Church in America began partly dependent on the Mother Church of Europe and partly independent. Finally all denominations were independent. Then they became independent with a vengeance. Everyone who discovered any phase of truth immediately organized it. An imp of

Satan came to his master very much disturbed and said, "Oh, what shall we do? A man on earth has discovered a portion of truth." "Never mind," said his Satanic Majesty, "I'll fix that. I'll get him to organize it." That would encase it and finally kill it. In America we have organized our truths into denominations. This has encased the truths, has kept them from getting over into other denominations. Sometimes the encasing has been very real, as in one denomination where it is called "spiritual adultery" even to set foot in the church of another denomination. American Christianity has achieved analysis, but it hasn't achieved synthesis. It has analyzed until it is paralyzed. It has picked the faith to pieces into special emphases, and now it doesn't know how to put it together into great inclusive affirmations. Therefore American Christianity is saying words to this generation instead of announcing the Word—the Word that gathers up all the lesser words into itself and goes beyond them. Instead of being a unifying force in American life the denominations have often been a divisive force— the one influence in small communities keeping the community apart. This is a sign of spiritual immaturity. Paul says: "I could not discuss things with you, my brothers, as spiritual persons; I had to address you as worldlings, as mere babes in Christ. I fed you with milk, not with solid food. . . . When one cries, 'I belong to Paul,' and another, 'I belong to Apollos,' what are you but men of the world?" (I Cor. 3:1-4—Moffatt.)

The question of how grown-up the American Church is will be decided in large measure by how quickly we can pass through these five stages to the final stage: (1) conflict, (2) competition, (3) comity, (4) co-operation, (5) federation,

(6) federal union. The Church is strung out in all of these stages, but it must move on, inevitably, to the final stage, federal union.

How soon this will be done will depend on the rediscovery of the Kingdom of God, for when once the Kingdom is discovered as central, then church federal union follows almost inevitably: "If I belong to the Kingdom of God, then all these lesser emphases of the Kingdom belong to me." The American Church will come to "new birth" if it comes to the "new man"—the new man out of all parties.

Again, the Church has failed to bring to a living synthesis evangelism and religious education, and largely for the same reason—its lack of the Kingdom as a framework in which it works. Without that all-encompassing framework which puts everything in its place, methods and emphases are lifted out of their proper perspective and become unbalanced—the part becomes the whole. There has been an estrangement between the movements of evangelism and religious education. They have been throwing gentle mud at each other—sometimes not so gentle! Evangelism says, "Life is crisis"; and religious education says, "Life is educational," unfolding, developmental. We are now seeing that life is both, that each emphasis is a half-truth. The Christian Church in China has put the two together in this statement: "Religious education will never be successful unless it is evangelistic, and evangelism will never be permanent unless it is educational." Religious education must provide for crisis conversion, for "the soul gets on by a series of crises"; evangelism must provide for educational methods, for without them the after-casualties in evangelism are great. If both evangelism and religious education will change and come to a third position beyond each, gathering up the truth in each into a living blend, then out of the two will emerge a new man; that will make peace. And it will not only make peace between movements, but will make them both a power. One without the other is weak; together they hit the total need.

Perhaps the Kingdom emphasis will yet bring together within the Christian Church the seemingly irreconcilable positions of pacifism and approval of war. The revolt against pacifism comes out of a confusion of it with passivism—a charge to which a great deal of pacifism has laid itself open. And the revolt against an approval of war, even as a "necessary necessity," comes from a legitimate insight that war and the Christian faith are irreconcilables. Suppose pacifism should be cleansed of its passivism by adding two things to its method: first the Gandhian method of nonviolent non-co-operation, which would make the method active and aggressive; and second the willingness to use an international police force to bring an aggressor before a bar of justice to be tried. That would fulfill the feeling of those who, very reluctantly approving of war, are convinced that we cannot refuse to do something; and that something may be force sufficient to bring an offender to a bar of justice. Between the Christian pacifist and those who believe it is right to settle things by war there is an irreconcilable difference. But there are very few who believe that. There is this difference between this war and other wars: nobody believes in this war! Even those who support it as a bad business that has to be gone through with know that this isn't the way. The possibility of a reconciliation on a higher level is not so remote, then, as it would seem. The new man out of both parties would be the man who would: (1) repudiate war as a method, (2) do everything possible to do away with the causes of war, (3) apply the Gandhian method wherever it could be applied, (4) be willing to approve of an international police force to bring offenders before an international tribunal of justice to be tried. But wouldn't the application of police force be the same as war? No. A police force uses enough force to bring the offender before a tribunal of right, but an army in war settles matters before a tribunal of might. This difference is profound and decisive; it allows us to accept one and reject the other. In the Kingdom God uses grace and judgment; the putting together of these four attitudes would do the same. The new man out of both parties would emerge. That would make peace between very widely conflicting views.

The lack of being possessed by the Christ-Kingdom emphasis has weakened the moral authority of the American pulpit. The finest introduction I have ever heard given to a speaker was given by a Negro minister: "The significance of Mahatma Gandhi is not in Gandhi as a person but in the fact that he is identified with a cause—the cause of India's freedom. When he speaks, the cause of India's freedom speaks. The significance of the speaker tonight is not in him as a person but in the fact that he is identified with a cause; when he speaks, the cause speaks. That cause is the Kingdom of God." It is just that lack of the authority of the divine Cause speaking through the minister that makes the pulpit utterances fall like a feather upon the conscience of this age. The minister is expressing an opinion instead of expressing a fact—the fact of God's Reign. It makes Chesterton's observation have point: "The world is filled with the knowledge of the last word, but knows nothing of the first word." It is from the standpoint of that "first word," "Seek ye first the Kingdom of God," that we must move out to every situation, to every person. We then come with an authority not our own; the Cause, the divine Order looks out of our eyes and speaks when we speak. The divine Government which stretches from the lowest cell to the farthest star comes to embodiment in us and speaks within our voice. "You are the new Order; it speaks when you speak," was a sincere compliment paid to a minister. Nothing finer could be said. And that is what men want to hear—divine authority. Some newspapermen said to me as I was about to address them: "Now don't talk *about* religion to us; talk religion." They wanted not an opinion about the fact; they wanted to feel the authority of the fact. Someone asked a Negro what was wrong with conditions in his community, and the reply was: "Well, the good ain't able, and the able ain't good." "The good ain't able"—goodness did not seem to be the eternally relevant and the inescapable; it could be put aside, and nothing happened.

During a discussion about the place of authority in Christianity one speaker used the phrase, "Our Sovereign God and Father," and a leading religious educationalist interrupting said, "I have no Sovereign," to which the speaker thoughtfully replied, "Then I pity you." He was right. A minister who doesn't begin with the awful sovereignty of the Kingdom of God is pitiable. Christ not embodying the Kingdom is just an attractive person, but Christ embodying that Kingdom is universal authority speaking.

I have been interested in going behind many pulpits

across the land to see what was behind the pulpit as giving a possible revelation of the man who habitually stands there. When I take hold of the edges of a pulpit I often find chewing gum stuck under them—the minister probably sticks it there during the prayer; I don't know when else he could do it! It revealed a chewing-gum type of mentality in the minister, probably producing a chewing-gum type of Christianity in the pew!

> A gum-chewing girl
> And a cud-chewing cow—
> There is a difference,
> I will allow.
> What is the difference?
> I have it now—
> It's the thoughtful look
> On the face of the cow!

Behind a good many pulpits you find a glass of water, with the implication that the minister is dry! Often we are, saying words out of which the content has dropped, repeating slogans that call us to nothing, preaching sermons instead of delivering messages. The pulpit does suffer from dryness.

Behind one pulpit I found a wastepaper basket, which I thought was good. Some of the sermons should have gone in before they went over! Every sermon that doesn't begin with the starting point, the Kingdom, should have an ending point, the wastebasket.

Behind one pulpit were some loose screws. Doesn't it show a sign of a screw loose somewhere when we preach about the last word, human relativisms, and neglect the first Word?

Behind one pulpit was a screwdriver. "Good," I said to myself. "That is what a minister should do—tighten up loose screws in his people!" And the Inner Voice answered, "Yes, and he should begin with himself and tighten up his own." The Voice sounded very *personal!*

Behind another pulpit I found a thermometer. "Good," I said again to myself. "Every minister should take his temperature as he goes into the pulpit to see whether this message has gone into his blood and has raised his temperature." To be the ambassador of the Kingdom of God—that should raise anyone's temperature. "Christ is in your blood," said a Hindu to me one day, and my inner comment was, "Well, if it is the living Christ, it is bound to raise my temperature." William James says, "Religion can be a dull habit or it can be an acute fever." Whether it is one or the other depends on whether we hold our message or our message holds us. "I should think you could keep six tongues going—you are bursting with things to say," said an African to a missionary visiting in Africa. He was trying to speak the unspeakable! "We cannot but speak the things which we have seen and heard," is the cry of the Christian who has once glimpsed the wonder of it all. Of Paul it was said by a scholar, "The Holy Ghost disorganized his grammar." No wonder, for the Word was bigger than his words!

Behind one pulpit—believe it or not—was a fire extinguisher! Since the minister and the service were the essence of propriety, it was probably not needed—no fire would break out in that pulpit! The whole thing lacked the divine spark. Someone prayed in a prayer meeting: "O God, grant that if any spark of divine grace has been kindled in this meeting—water that spark." The modern Church has been praying that prayer; it has been watering sparks.

We are suffering from a toned-down Christianity. An Englishman traveling through New England in the autumn and seeing the flaming reds of the maples remarked, "Don't you think it is a little overdone?" He felt that the Creator had lacked restraint—it was overdone! Speaking of New England reminds me of a New England Congregationalist in one of our Ashrams who said, "I belong to God's frozen people." A great deal of American Christianity is lukewarm, if not frozen. The tragedy of American Christianity is that it has lost the consciousness of its birthday, Pentecost. The teaching concerning, and the fact of, the Holy Spirit has been pushed to the edges of American Christianity, been pushed into the marginal denominations. The consequence is that Pentecost is identified with the marginal—sometimes with the queer—to the spiritual impoverishment of the main stream of Christianity. For without the Holy Spirit the Christian faith is outside of you in history; it is faith in a Person who lived and died and arose; it is historical but it is not experimental. Jesus said the Holy Spirit is *with* you, and shall be *in* you." American Christianity impresses one as being a religion of "with" instead of "in": God is "with" people, illuminating and inspiring now and then, fitfully; but he is not deeply within, "a well of water spring up into everlasting life." American Christianity is largely artificial instead of artesian.

The modern minister and the modern church are to be seen in Apollos and the church at Ephesus. Apollos was "a man of culture, strong in his knowledge of the scriptures. He . . . taught about Jesus with ardor and accuracy, though all the baptism he knew was that of John." (Acts 18:24-25—Moffatt.) But the baptism of John was the gospel of a demand, "Don't do this," "Do that"—a whipping up of the moral will. The total picture of this minister, then, is that of a cultured, well-informed, earnest, meticulous man laying a moral demand on the unreinforced wills of those whom he served. Result? When Paul visited the Ephesian congregation he found "twelve" disciples (Acts 19:7) made into the image of their minister—twelve men ineffective, noncontagious, pathetically striving in their own strength to be Christian. The other group of twelve disciples were turning the world upside down; this group of twelve were huddled together for mutual protection.

Why was one group of twelve men an issue, a contagion, an irresistible movement, and the other easily set aside as irrelevant, without the spark of contagion—a congregation instead of a movement? Paul sensed the reason when he put the question: "Did you receive the Holy Spirit?" And they had not. One group had received the Holy Spirit, and the other had not. The difference was profound, decisive. When they did receive the Holy Spirit, the tide turned; the city was stirred to its depths; "awe fell on them all"; books of magic were publicly burned—"Thus did the word of the Lord increase and prevail mightily." (Acts 19:3, 17-20—Moffatt.) From a turned-in, on-the-defensive type of Christianity they became turned out, on the offensive, radiant, redemptive. So deep became their Christianity that Paul, when he wrote his epistle to them, was stretched to his depths to place before them his profoundest conceptions of the Christian faith. Had they been shallow, Paul would have been compelled to talk surface things to them, but they were capable of taking the profoundest, and as a result we and the rest of the world have been profoundly enriched by the epistle that unfolds "the Breadth," "the Length," "the Depth," "the Height" of the gospel. (Eph. 3:18, 19— Moffatt.) The Holy Spirit was no longer *with* them; he was *in* them, and the difference was the difference between a copyist and a creative type of spiritual life.

As I go about the American churches I feel the lack of spiritual radiance and power; they are more akin to the Ephesus of Apollos than to the Ephesus of Paul, more like the twelve of Ephesus than the twelve of Jerusalem. In American Christianity you do not feel the Holy Spirit capitalizing all our common nouns and changing mere numerals into a multiplying force. A strong fundamentalist said to a very able minister: "Doctor, you know everything about Christianity except one thing: you don't know how to help a man to be a Christian." The minister did not become angry, for it was true; he did know everything except just *that,* and that *that* was everything.

American Christianity, in by-passing Pentecost, trying to go from the life and teachings of Christ to world conquest without the inner reinforcement and unifying power which the Holy Spirit brings, has found itself spiritually inadequate, exhausting itself upon the problems of the day. It must beat a strategic retreat, a retreat back to its own resources; and then it will go further; it will go anywhere. For when the Holy Spirit moves into the center of your being, the word "How?" is answered. And that is the word the modern man wants to hear answered. He is convinced of the "What?" and the "Why?" He wants to know "How?" Not to answer that word "How?" or to try to answer it by emphasizing all the more the words "What?" and "Why?" leaves the modern man baffled and frustrated. In Batavia, New York, the citizens put in a $40,000 swimming pool and then found after dedication there wasn't a pipe leading into it; the purpose for which it was put up was left out. It was a wonderful swimming pool, but it had no water! The modern Church has everything—culture, eloquence, knowledge— everything except "a well of water springing up into ever-lasting life."

To change the figure, the heartbeat of the Church is feeble. Abundant spiritual vitality doesn't seem to be coursing through its veins. Spiritually it is below par. All the organs are there, all the framework of living is present, but it lacks—life! A rather absent-minded missionary traveled 250 miles to Bombay to get her watch fixed; it wouldn't run. The watchmaker looked it over, wound it up, and handed it back to her. There was nothing wrong with it except it wasn't wound. Modern Christianity needs to be wound; it needs an inner spring, something to make it go. It needs Pentecost.

I would redeem that word "Pentecost." It is now bound up in the thinking of many with rampant emotionalism and outmoded thinking. In a great mass meeting opening the National Christian Mission in a Southern city, the man who gave the opening prayer prayed that "this might be another Pentecost." As I stood up to read, I found on the Bible a letter addressed to me wishing us well as we began the Mission and containing a rabbit's foot. I said to the audience that Pentecost and rabbits' feet—high emotion and low intelligence—had very often been linked together in American Christianity. And many, in throwing away the rabbit's-foot expression of Christianity had thrown away Pentecost too. To change the figure, they had "thrown away the baby with the bath water."

Jesus said: "There be some of them that stand here, which shall not taste of death, till they have seen the Kingdom of God come with power." They did see the Kingdom of God come with power—at Pentecost, where timid believers became irresistible apostles; where ambitious and unintegrated individuals became a community, became a fellowship; where the economic and the racial were brought under a new control and given a new direction, the direction of equality of opportunity for all; where Christianity broke the fetters of Judaism and became universalized; where Christianity passed from being a "counsel of perfection" into being a "counsel of possibility," here and now; where the ordinary became the extraordinary; where all life was lifted from the sordid to the sacred; where God and his resources moved on the inside, a fountain within; where the believer was no longer wistful, but winsome; where the individual and the group, hitherto dead metal, were magnetized with a divine magnetism, drawing loose and purposeless and directionless humanity to themselves as a magnet draws iron filings; where dead-hearted men became alive with a gay and purposeful joy; where piety was natural and spontaneous; where there was "a holiness of the natural and a naturalness of the holy"; where life was Life!

The American Church needs *that!*

Chapter XVI—
WHAT OF THE FUTURE?

AMERICAN CHRISTIANITY HAS now grown up; it is not yet mature, but it is of age. It need no longer imitate; it can be itself. It can learn from Europe and Asia and Africa and incorporate into its interpretation what it can assimilate usefully and beneficially. But from henceforth let American Christianity be American Christianity. It is not Christianity; we do not arrogate our interpretation of Christianity into Christianity itself. It is only an interpretation. I use interpreters a good deal, and interpretation from one language into another has been defined as "the compound fracture of an idea, with immediate mortification setting in." The passing of Christianity from Palestine to Europe to America is literally the compound fracture of an idea, and when we view the result immediate mortification very often does set in. And yet the matter works the other way: the passing of an idea from one civilization to another may enrich instead of impoverish, may fructify instead of fracture. We hope that the passing of Christianity through American civilization will transform and enrich that civilization and at the same time enrich the world interpretation of that Christianity.

We will not shut ourselves off from other national interpretations. How can we? We will receive with gratitude the interpretation of British Christianity with its emphasis upon the continuity and the solidarity of the centuries; the Continental interpretation with its emphasis upon the "otherness" of God and the invasion of the divine from without; the Russian interpretation with its social passion and willingness to sacrifice for a cause; the Indian interpretation with its deep mysticism and its emphasis upon oneness with the Divine; the Chinese with its matter-of-fact concreteness in spiritual things; the Japanese with its disciplined art and capacity for loyalty; the African with its deep sense of rhythm and spiritual gaiety; the Latin American with its love of the beautiful and its all-inclusive racial attitudes—all these are differing strings across which God sweeps the bow of his purposes to bring out a fuller and more rounded harmony. We shall take what we can from others, but we shall no longer be afraid to be *ourselves*. For in being ourselves we are everybody else, for the world is in our national veins. And yet we are not a mere conglomeration; we are a new man, a new man out of all parties. We will now dare to be that new man and humbly and simply offer our contribution to the world. We will not copy; we will create.

Roland Hayes, the Negro singer, says: "I was working in a cloud of depression because my voice had not come out as 'white' as in the beginning I had hoped it would. Now I swore I would use the 'rich purplish red' that Nature had given me. I felt a great release from nervous tension, and at the same time a kind of exultation. . . . I could be myself, sole, personal, unique." That is a second Emancipation Proclamation—freedom to be oneself without pride or arrogance, in fact, with deep humility. The voice of America will never come out "English" or "Continental." Let it come out the "rich purplish red" of the American heritage and outlook. Let American Christianity be American Christianity, and by doing so it can more nearly be world Christianity. Just as I say to India and China, "You have a right to go past us straight to the New Testament, and there let the love and power of Christ play upon your national soul and out of that firsthand contact give your unique interpretation, and we will sit at your feet in gratitude," so I would say the same to America: "Let God pull out the stops and play you all over."

Strangely enough—and yet not strangely—the most characteristic American philosophy was uttered not by John Dewey, though he came close to uttering it, but by an American Negro, Dr. George Carver. "I have stumbled on a new philosophy of life which has transformed me. How I wish I had stumbled on it sooner!" said an Army chaplain to me in one of the camps. It was the simple but penetrating philosophy of Carver: "Take what you have and make something out of it." In other words, don't spend your time in useless crying for what you haven't got; don't cry for the moon; take what you have and make something out of it. His illustration, frequently used, was that of the sailors dying of thirst in an open boat when one of them in desperation dipped down and took up some of the water and drank it and found it was sweet; they had drifted into the wide, open mouth of the Amazon River. "Dip up the water where you are," says Carver. He did. He took what the South had, clay, sweet potatoes, and peanuts, and out of clay made paints and other things, out of sweet potatoes made 150 commercial products, and out of peanuts 300 commercial products.

Every time I see a lowly sweet potato or a still more lowly peanut I now feel like tipping my hat to it. Carver made the low-caste into high-caste. I said to him, "Dr. Carver, you and I are in the same great business. You are discovering wonders in peanuts, and I'm discovering wonders in people, both of them wrapped in strange wrappings."

American Christianity must take what it has—the American heritage and characteristics—and make something out of them. We must offer to God the raw materials of our heritage and accomplishments so that together we may produce an American interpretation of the Kingdom of God.

Just what have we to offer? Even the best we have needs cleansing, but perhaps in the very act of putting it at the disposal of God there will be a cleansing. I would suggest twelve things as constituting what we have to offer.

1. *Materialism*. The most obvious thing about us is that we have been and are a materialistically-minded people. We will have to accept that as a fact and make something out of it. We cannot renounce this whole material civilization and turn back in our repentance to a bed of spikes like the Hindu sadhu. We must take materialism and make something out of it. For there is a core of good in materialism. The Christian believes in the material; it is God-made, and what is God-made cannot be wrong. Moreover we believe in an incarnation—the manifestation of the divine in terms material. Then let our materialism be cleansed and guided. We must not merely spiritualize the material; we must materialize the spiritual. We must make the spiritual function in terms of matter; we must literally materialize it. Instead of our materialism's being an expression of selfish-

240

ness, it will then be an expression of our Christian faith. How? (1) We must distribute our material wealth widely; we must not allow it to get into the hands of the few to the impoverishment of the many. "Luxuries are the things that make people go without necessities." (2) Our materialism must express quality instead of mere quantity; it must be the incarnation of the beautiful, the necessary, the beneficial; it must meet our aesthetic, our economic, our social needs. Instead of having a mere body it must have a soul. If "work is love made visible," then our materialism should be love made visible—love of the beautiful, love of the underprivileged, love of the brotherhood, love of the creative.

2. *Our love of success.* The youth who objected to my remark that American youth has no cause by saying it has one—"We want to succeed"—put his finger on the central desire of our civilization, the desire for success. We cannot reverse that will to live successfully; we must accept it and redirect it, redirect it toward greater and nobler ends. We have said that a man succeeds to the degree that he accumulates; this is a false success, for such success may have meant the failure of others. Let our success be harnessed to the collective good—we succeed only as we help others to succeed. In helping others to succeed, then, it redounds in real success in us; we grow tall in helping others to their feet. The drive of the success motive must be detached from individual self-centeredness and attached to the public good —to the making of a society where the success of one is the success of all and the success of all is the success of the one. Then success will be redeemed. Now success is not redemptive; it is destructive. Out of one hundred healthy men

at the age of twenty-six, at the age of sixty-five one will be rich, four fairly prosperous, five will be supporting themselves, thirty-six will be dead, and fifty-four will be dependent on relatives, friends, or charity. There is something wrong when there is this ultimate wreckage. A dog-eat-dog economy must be replaced by a society of mutual aid. Success must be success only as it helps oneself and others to succeed.

3. *Nervous energy.* We are a people with a vast amount of nervous energy. That nervous energy, because it is not harnessed to great ends, is making us a jittery people. The patron saint of America is St. Vitus! Her sign is the jumpy, jittery neon sign! The result is that seventy-five per cent of the patients in our public hospitals are psychopathic patients—people who have cracked under the strain of disjointed or purposeless nervous tension. I have repeated Jesus' words: "Keep your loins girt and your lamps lit." America has her loins girt, ready for ceaseless activity, but her lamps are not lit. Hence there is a lot of stumbling about in the dark, knocking our shins against the system of things. Our lamps must be lit; we must see where we're going; we must direct this nervous energy to ends that really count, for ourselves and others. We must harness this nervous energy to reconstruction at home and abroad. For unharnessed it is a flood, destroying itself and others; harnessed it turns turbines that produce electricity, which in turn gives light and power. American nervous energy is the world's greatest liability—also the world's greatest asset. We must harness it to world reconstruction.

4. *Our capacity for mass production.* This is revolutionary. Our industrial economy is now geared to an economy of

abundance for everybody. We have now the machinery, the techniques, the knowledge to raise the economic level of the life of everybody in America and in the world. If myopic self-interest rules it, we will slow down production, slaughter pigs, plow under crops, and try to keep up the prices for the benefit of the few. If we can put behind this mass production a spirit of loving your neighbor as you love yourself, then we can let this mass production run at full blast without any brakes on it, for the world is suffering for goods of every kind. Let mass production become production for the masses—the masses at home and abroad, the masses everywhere. Then mass production will be redeemed and will, in being redeemed, have an open door.

5. *We are the people of a frontier mind.* Our outstanding leaders have been frontiersmen—Washington by choice, Jefferson in Virginia, Lincoln in Illinois, Jackson in Tennessee, Theodore Roosevelt in South Dakota. We are the people who love to push our minds and bodies against the unknown and the unexplored. And now some men say that all the frontiers are closed and we must "settle down to a mature civilization." Must we? Are all the frontiers closed? They are not closed; they are simply changing; they are now economic, social, and spiritual instead of geographic. Let the frontier spirit of America go up against the frontier problem of our Negro citizens—discriminated against, suppressed, and segregated. There is a frontier problem worthy of our moral and spiritual hardihood and capacity to solve the difficult. And the frontier of poverty among the masses at home, plus the frontiers of ignorance, of disease, of poverty abroad. These are the new frontiers calling to the daring in our manhood and womanhood. Let us offer our frontier

spirit to God to tackle new frontiers at home and abroad.

6. *Our belief in man.* The central genius of our democracy is our faith in man as a man. Given the facts, we say, in the long run man will do the right thing. It is the most stimulating and dynamic thing, humanly speaking, in our civilization. For the people who influence you are the people who believe in you; you feel you must rise to their expectations.

Let us take that faith in man and apply it to man as man everywhere. First of all to everybody in our own midst. Let us go out to stimulate everybody and throw open the doors of equal opportunity to every single person. We must galvanize beaten people and make them have a faith in God, in themselves and in the future. This would apply to the Negro, the Japanese-American, the Mexican in our midst, and the American Indian. We can drive them, by our attitudes, into segregations and a sense of inferiority; or we can inspire and stimulate and assimilate. And this faith in man would apply to people outside of our own borders. If the cynicisms and critical attitudes toward subject people, so characteristic of imperialism, bite into our souls, we are poisoned, fatally poisoned; democracy with its creative belief in man dies within us. But faith creates faith and creates possibilities. Let us keep our faith in people—in people everywhere.

7. *Our respect for women.* America has been called "a woman's paradise." But our respect for woman has been misdirected. We have set woman on a pedestal, or we have acquiesced as she has tried to imitate us. Both are false attitudes. Woman should be expected to make her own distinctive contribution, which only she as a woman can make.

That distinctive contribution is to produce a co-operative order. If, as Benjamin Kidd says, women are to be "the psychic center of power in the future," because they represent the co-operative spirit and the future belongs to co-operation, then why not encourage and inspire women to be true to that call and give themselves to produce that co-operative order? Propaganda, mostly in the hands of men, has been directed to make women over into our ugly image —to smoke as many cigarettes, to swill as much liquor, to wear as many pants, to be a second-rate copy of ourselves. If a man who has womanish characteristics is called a "sissie"—a term of reproach—then why isn't a woman who tries to have mannish characteristics called a "brussie"—also a term of reproach? Let both men and women be themselves and make their distinctive contribution. And let woman be true to her call and destiny and give herself to produce a co-operative order. For it is desperately needed.

8. *Our good nature.* The American is the best-tempered man on earth. And I say that deliberately. After coming back from other lands where things get on mostly by jawing and tongue-lashing and abuse, I went across America for a year and a half and could not remember that I had seen a single person speaking in an abusive tone to anyone. Why? Well, for one reason, they didn't dare to! The employer who abused his employees would lose them! We get angry only with those who have no comeback; when we have to hold our temper we do. So we do! This has created a national habit of good temper and good will. A car in which I was riding stalled in the midst of traffic, and a policeman strode over. We waited for the storm. Instead he put his head in the window and said, "I've got a car

that does exactly the same thing." I could have hugged him!

And now that unfailing good temper must be harnessed to the needs of a world frayed to its depths with bad temper and conflict. We must become a reconciling power in an estranged world. Our function in world affairs is not to carry the big stick but the big sticking-plaster, to bind up the gaping wounds of a bleeding world. "Thank you for what you are trying to do," said Admiral Nomura, the Japanese Ambassador. "You are trying to reconcile us, and anyone who is trying to reconcile others is doing the work of Heaven, for it is Heaven's work to reconcile us." I was deeply moved—a non-Christian telling me, a Christian, what my chief business was, to reconcile. And that is America's chief business. Imperialisms may bluster and threaten; our democracy must reconcile and reconstruct.

9. *Pragmatism.* We have a profound faith in the thing that works. That has its weaknesses, for pragmatism as a philosophy of life lacks depth. But there is a truth in pragmatism, and a very valuable one. Let us boldly apply it to a philosophy of life that does have depth and universal validity—the Christian philosophy. Let us put the Christian way under the test of life to see if life will approve it—to see whether it will work. Let the rest of the world speculate and philosophize; that is not our genius. Let us test, try, prove, verify under actual life. If we are going to be pragmatic, let us be pragmatic in the supreme business—the business of living. If the Christian way is our best bet, our most likely hypothesis, let us relentlessly put it to the test— the test in the total life, individual and collective. There we have the possibility of being a demonstration ground of the worth-whileness and workability of the Christian way. We

will find it works in every conceivable circumstance and in every sphere. And we will find that it is the only thing that does work. For the universe has a way written into it, and that way is the Christian way. Never before have we had a pragmatic people with world power, in a strategic world position, who could do what America can now do, namely, demonstrate in actual life before the eyes of a confused world the sheer practicability of the Christian way. America, with her pragmatic genius, has come to the Kingdom for such a time as this. For old ways of life are cracking and breaking down under the pressure of the demands of life. There is only one way that will work—God's way, the Christian way.

10. *Love of freedom.* The essential American note is the love of freedom. It is the note that brings light to the eye, quickens the pulse, and possesses the being with complete consent. America and freedom are synonymous.

Then since we give ourselves to it, let us do so completely. Let our love of freedom be a love of freedom for *all*. Those who love freedom for some—white people, people of a certain class, of a certain creed—these do not love freedom. They want freedom to exploit, to use others as means to their ends; they are the wolves of selfishness in the sheeps' clothing of freedom.

The next great step in our manifestation of our love of freedom is to go out on a crusade to make all men free, everywhere—and this regardless of color, race, class, or creed. This crusade would sweep all imperialisms from the earth, all exploitation of class by class, of sex by sex, of person by person. That would prove our love of freedom and would put reality into our pledge of allegiance to the flag of "one Nation, indivisible, with liberty and justice for *all*," for we would mean the "all." Otherwise we will be saying in essence what one boy was found saying when he repeated the pledge: ". . . one naked individual, with liberty and just sticks for all." Our national emasculation of the pledge in actuality is not less ridiculous than the little boy's when we turn liberty and justice for "all" into "liberty and justice for some." Let our love of freedom be love of freedom for all, everywhere.

11. *Our love of variety.* The expression of our central genius, we have insisted, is *"E pluribus unum"*—"Out of the many one." This is what we have been raised up to illustrate and to give to the rest of the world. And nothing is more desperately needed; for if, in our struggle for a unified world, we try to get unity through uniformity and a jamming of everyone into a certain mold of our choosing, then instead of unity we will get resistance and consequent chaos. We should appreciate diversity and encourage it and use it, and then unify it without sacrificing the diversity. Then and then only will we have peace and progress and an open door.

As we have found unity amid diversity in our own land, let us put this at the disposal of the rest of the world, refusing all special alliances, refusing all racialisms, but holding ourselves open to be the instrument of God to bring a larger world unity through a federal union of the world. That is our national destiny.

12. *Faith in the future.* The people who founded this country were the people of the future. They had turned their backs upon the past—not entirely, of course, for that past was in their blood and bone, and thus inescapable, and

yet they were the people of the great faith, the great faith in the future. If we let go that simple faith in the future and become bitter with cynicism about man and his future, we shall write "Finis" upon the great experiment. A little hunchback Y.M.C.A. secretary, with little knowledge of the Near East but with an amazing faith in people, went into static Turkey believing that people would do anything; and in response to his amazing faith in them the Turks did do what he expected of them. They had faith in his faith. He rescued 200,000 Greeks in the debacle at Smyrna and was decorated by both the Greeks and the Turks; both sides loved the man of faith. In the spirit of that little man America must meet the future at home and abroad; she must go out to inspire faith in bosoms where it has died, to help stricken peoples to their feet, to open the doors of equal opportunity to every last mother's son on earth, to fight against disease, ignorance, poverty, inequalities everywhere. The future of the world is in the hands of believers. The nonbelievers cannot act: they cancel themselves out by doubt and dilemma. We must be the people, not of a No, but of a Yes. We must live by great affirmations about God and man and the future.

These are the twelve things we have to offer to the world —the twelve apostles of the spirit of America: our cleansed and redirected materialism, our love of success, our nervous energy, our capacity for mass production, our frontier spirit, our belief in man, our respect for women, our unquenchable good will, our pragmatic mind, our love of freedom, our belief in unity amid variety, and our faith in the future. In the words of that great American, Carver, we will "take what we have and make something out of them." Or better, like the little boy with the five loaves and two fishes we will turn over into the hands of Christ our Master and Leader these twelve possibilities for him to bless, to break, and then to distribute and thus feed the hungry multitudes. We are deeply conscious that before he can use these qualities they must be cleansed, but perhaps in the very offering of them to him they will be cleansed.

But behind and beyond and above all these possibilities stands the author, and we trust the finisher, of the best in them—the Christ of the American Road. If we must interpret him to the world through these qualities, we know that he stands greater than his interpreters and greater than the interpretation. If the world finds it difficult to take these twelve qualities because "Made in U.S.A." is stamped on them, we are still not nonplused and frustrated, for we have this Christ himself to offer. We have to apologize for ourselves, for we are "only Christians in the making"; for our country, for it is only partially Christianized; for the Church, for it too is only partly expressive of his Spirit; but concerning him we have no apologies to make. In regard to him there are no apologies on our lips, for there are none in our hearts. He is the author of all that is worthwhile in our civilization; his stamp is upon all of our goodness, and his redemption is upon our sins and weaknesses. And, we gratefully add, he is not American. He is the universal Christ who belongs to all men of all climes, of all races—the Son of Man. As a part of the sons of men we have tried to interpret this Son of Man—an imperfect interpretation we know, for we the interpreters are very, very imperfect; but it is the best we have and we offer our interpretation to the rest of the world. If others will take this universal Christ and will through their own genius show us a better interpretation, we will sit at their feet. For we do not worship our interpretation; we worship and follow the Christ who is bigger than our interpretation. He is the best we have; we know nothing better, and we can be content with nothing less.

The day the attack on Pearl Harbor took place I was coming down the steps of a hotel in Urbana, Illinois, on my way to speak to a mass meeting of students of the university on "The Basis of a Just and Lasting Peace" when I heard the radio announcer telling in excited tones of the attack that precipitated the war. I had tried for months as a go-between to head off this conflict, and here it was upon us. The world I had tried, with others, to build up had crashed. And here I was on my way to speak on the basis of a lasting peace—and peace was gone! I announced to the meeting what I had heard over the radio, and added that it was obviously impossible to speak on the subject announced, for peace was gone, but I would speak to them instead on "What Christ Means to Me." Amid the crashing of the world of peace we had tried to build up, I found that all my values upon which I had staked my life were intact: Christ was still there intact; my real world was unshaken, and moreover unshakable. That afternoon a thousand students stayed in the after-meeting to find this Christ in a personal way. The center of my universe held intact then at the war's beginning, and it holds now during the war's continuance, and at the war's end there will be One standing on the horizon—the one hope of our shattered humanity. "See the Christ stand!"

If I were to pick out a symbol of America which I would like to see placed upon our coins and on our seals, I would pick out the sequoia tree, the big tree of the West Coast, a native of our soil and the oldest living thing on our planet. Why has this tree existed through the ages, from two to four thousand years, surviving the rise and fall of empires and nations? The secret of its survival has been sixfold: (1) *It is straight;* had it been crooked the law of gravitation which holds it up in its straightness would have pulled it to the earth in its crookedness. (2) *It stays itself up on the side that is weak;* it puts out a stay and props itself up on the side that has any tendency to lean. (3) *It has power to resist small enemies;* borers do not like its bark or fiber because of an acid within. (4) *It has a power of self-healing when deeply hurt and scarred;* it throws scar tissue, burl, around its wounds and heals them over. (5) *It puts up a new top if the old is struck off by lightning;* one of the branches turns upward, the strength of the rest goes into it, and a new top is formed; it keeps on growing. (6) *It belongs to a society of mutual aid;* its roots are not deep, there is no central taproot; but the trees live in clumps, their roots intertwine, and they hold each other up. For these six reasons these great handiworks of God—for "only God can make a tree"—have stood amid the decay and ruin of the centuries.

We as individuals and as a nation will stand undecaying amid the decay of individuals and civilizations *provided* we are straight; the laws of the Kingdom of God will hold us up, but if we get out of alignment with those laws the same laws that would hold us up now will pull us to the dust, for only those who do the will of God abide forever; the rest perish. We will stand *provided* we have the intelligent foresight and moral courage to put down stays that strengthen us against a tendency to lean in certain directions: toward unequal privileges of capital against the laborer, toward giving privileges to white people denied to colored people, toward making our government work in behalf of the party in power instead of for the good of the people, toward selfish interests because they can pay for special privileges, toward men as against equal rights and privileges to women—we must stay ourselves against leaning in any direction anywhere. We will stand *provided* we have within us the capacity to throw off small enemies, little borers that eat away the substance of character: snobberies that would give liberty and justice to some but not to all, regardless of class and race and color; selfishness that would love ourselves but not our neighbors as ourselves; cynicisms that eat out faith and confidence; dishonesties with ourselves and others; a lack of imaginative sympathy that can put ourself in the other person's place. We will stand *provided* we have within us the power to heal over the great wounds of life with the scar tissue, the burl, of the great redemptive grace of God, the power of our inner recovery from shocks and divisions and conflicts and lapses in character—a redemptive, restorative force within us making us strong where we are weak, brave where we are cowardly, self-giving where we are selfish, victorious where we are defeated. We will stand *provided,* when we meet catastrophe —a lightning bolt that would knock off our top as it reaches ever higher in aspiration and would stop any further growth —we can have the undiscouraged dynamic within us that would put out a new top, that would refuse to believe that we cannot recover and grow taller, that lives by mighty affirmations and faith when people begin to croak that we have reached the limit of development, that never knows when it is beaten, that forever pushes its head higher into God's eternal blue, that knows how to live "in spite of" when it cannot live "on account of." We will stand *provided* we let our roots intertwine and hold each other up, the strength of each being the strength of all and the strength of all being the strength of each—a society of mutual aid; for if we try to stand out alone with no responsibility for others, taking care of ourselves alone, then nature will take care that we are laid alone in the dust; from sheer necessity we must co-operate or perish; we must decide that the roots of capital and labor, the white man and the colored, America and the rest of the world, should and must intertwine and hold each other up against the storms of life—then we shall live; all of us shall live, for we shall live for all.

Then shall the central genius of America, *"E pluribus unum"*—"Out of the many one"—come to fulfillment, the fulfillment of the American dream; and then shall come into realization the central genius of our Christian faith—the production of a new man out of both parties, so making peace. Then shall our Christ and our country, now no longer at cross-purposes, work together to fulfill the American dream—and more, to bring into realization the Kingdom of God and to make our very land in some real measure a miniature of that Kingdom.

But if this is done, then individually and collectively we must submit to and obey, as our Saviour and Lord and Leader, the Christ of the American Road.

But perhaps my reader says with a sigh, "Suppose

'collectively' we are not willing and prepared to submit to and obey this Christ of the American Road, are all our hopes canceled?" No! For across the ages sounds again the word of this Christ: "Fear not, little flock; for it is your Father's good pleasure to give you the Kingdom." The little flock, the small minority, can be the agent of the coming of that Kingdom. For as we look back across our national history we find that all the great changes for the better have come through small minorities—small minorities that had a cause and were dedicated, disciplined, and determined. We too have a Cause—the Cause of causes, the Kingdom of God. And further, we have a Leader who embodies that Cause; the Leader and the Order coincide; and if we too, though a little flock, are dedicated, disciplined, and determined, then we may be the agent of the coming of that Kingdom, provided we are prepared to submit to and obey the Christ of the American Road.